D1532374

THE AGRARIAN
TRANSITION
IN AMERICA

DUALISM
AND
CHANGE

THE AGRARIAN
TRANSITION
IN AMERICA

DUALISM
AND
CHANGE

WAYNE C. ROHRER
LOUIS H. DOUGLAS
Kansas State University

THE BOBBS-MERRILL COMPANY, INC.
A SUBSIDIARY OF HOWARD W. SAMS & CO., INC.
INDIANAPOLIS • NEW YORK

ROBERT McGINNIS
Consulting Editor
Cornell University

Copyright © 1969 by the Bobbs-Merrill Company, Inc.
Printed in the United States of America
Library of Congress Catalog Card Number 68–15586
First Printing

PREFACE

The transition of agriculture is a widely sought objective
of this time. In simplest terms, the transition means that farm
productivity will be increased to obtain surplus production.
Further, it means that increasing farm production will
free even more people from farming. The occupation of
larger fractions of the labor force in nonfarm pursuits becomes
possible as fewer are employed in producing food. One
can say that a successfully executed transition contributes
to an industrializing economy and an urbanizing society.

The definition specified above, while succinct, is overly
simple. This qualification is borne out in the following
chapters. In the American context, developing the means to
provide surplus food to an urban-industrial population, to free
farm natives for urban employment, and to obtain products
for export required numerous private and public inputs,
an extensive time period, the development of elaborate
organizational structures, and the taking of many steps that
were not readily or widely accepted. However, the American
case illustrates one route traversed in this quest. Perhaps
others will discover promising paths or learn of the
consequences of certain courses by reviewing our account.

The transition of agriculture, in nation after nation, has
taken off (or will take off) from the terminal of peasant
farming. The peasant style of life has ramified throughout
the economy, polity, and society of the nations in
which it is found. Any concern with changing this
way of life has been subjected to passionate expression
and close scrutiny. Moreover, many observers—policy-makers,
scientists, men of letters—act to resist or to implement
changes of the peasantry.

We have chosen specimen remarks from a few observers
to elucidate the stifled transition, the transition under way,
and one social consequence of the transformation of

agriculture. Lowry Nelson, a sociologist, noted within the decade prior to Castro's revolution:

Political unrest, arising from the frustration of the desire of peasants to obtain possession of and security on the land, will be chronic in Cuba until more positive action is taken in this respect. Admittedly the problem is a difficult one, with the existing rights of large landholders to consider; but it is not a question that can be continually postponed. It is likely that continued delay in carrying out the law may result in serious political consequences.[1]

That land reform had been thwarted was apparently a cardinal impetus to the revolution that followed a few years after Nelson's work was published. The framework for implementing evolutionary change was available but the implementation of land reform was resisted by well-placed Cubans. We would not argue that a freeholding peasantry is a precondition to enter on the transition. However, land reform would have encouraged the choice of a democratic option in transforming agriculture in preference to a totalitarian option. Resisting land reform was a sufficient if not a necessary precondition for the choice of revolutionary change.

Oliver Goldsmith's references to "Sweet Auburn" indicate the passion with which intellectuals who were negatively disposed to the transition viewed this change. For example:

Ill fares the land, to hastening ills a prey,
Where wealth accumulates, and men decay.
Princes and lords may flourish, or may fade;
A breath can make them, as a breath has made:
But a bold peasantry, their country's pride,
When once destroy'd, can never be supplied.[2]

Goldsmith viewed the transition at its onset in the first nation to become industrialized. The cited passage assuredly underscores the virtues of rural living and more.
The peasantry was sui generis.

---

[1] Lowry Nelson, *Rural Cuba* (Minneapolis: University of Minnesota Press, 1950), p. 255.
[2] "The Deserted Village," *Harvard Classics: English Poetry, Two* (New York: P. F. Collier & Son, 1910), pp. 522-523.

Thus the farming class was more than a fundamental social aggregate: Peasants were uniquely capable of provisioning the larger society.

One way the contemporary world may be distinguished from the era of Goldsmith is that many observers regard the peasantry and farming in a different light. For example, the following excerpts from an economist's article on collective agriculture:

Czechoslovak agriculture is going through not only a social and economic, but also a technical revolution. This can be seen in the way new techniques are reaching into agriculture and in the way motor-driven power is being substituted more and more for animal draught power and manpower. . . . Since we are directing production in industry toward new technique, the same applies of course to agriculture in our country. Agriculture will obtain this technique from industry, so it's up to our engineering industry to equip agriculture with really first-class and highly efficient technique.[3]

Agriculture does not have a unique quality in this view. Farming constitutes an industrial process. It relies on engineers to implement the transition to increased productivity. Although Goldsmith and Mysliveček assume different stances in viewing agriculture, they are ironically alike in attributing uniqueness to a single social aggregate. The onset of the transition of agriculture, whether it is cast in an economic context of eighteenth-century laissez faire or twentieth-century collectivism, is characterized by social strain and/or change.

Restudy of an American farm community—Plainville— by Art Gallaher provides us with a reference that specifies the following consequence of the agricultural transition.

Ours is an economy with an embarrassing agricultural surplus. The latter is tied to a rapidly expanding technology. This technology, though adaptable to the family farm if used successfully and efficiently, demands the imperatives [more

---

[3]Fr. Mysliveček, "Development of Czechoslovak Agriculture Under the Third Five-Year Plan," *For Socialist Agricultural Science*, X, No. 1 (1961), 18.

land, more livestock, increased mechanization, more capital, and greater management skill] previously mentioned. This in turn renders an archaic farmer, or one limited by land resources, ineffective in his efforts to sustain a desirable level of living on a family-size unit.[4]

In other words, if we view the transition of agriculture wholly as a process of rationalizing production, America at this point in time has a success on its hands. However, this success has yielded an aggregate of farmers, termed the excluded segment or refugists in later chapters, who do not and/or cannot practice modern agriculture. The transition in America has had this by-product.

[4]Art Gallaher, Jr., *Plainville: Fifteen Years Later* (New York: Columbia University Press, 1961), p. 258.

ACKNOWLEDGMENTS

This work bears a direct relationship to an interdisciplinary, interagency activity of Kansas State University that was called Area Development. The Area Development activity had evolved out of a series of seminars concerning the future of agriculture that had been funded by the College of Agriculture of Kansas State.

The authors are particularly and deeply indebted to Dr. C. Peairs Wilson, Dean, College of Tropical Agriculture, University of Hawaii, who, as Director of the Kansas Agricultural Experiment Station, encouraged, advised, counseled, and supported social research generally and our research efforts and interests specifically. Vice President Glenn H. Beck was also supportive in the implementation of the work in Area Development. We are grateful for his advice and assistance. Administrators of the agricultural programs of land-grant universities have not always so willingly sponsored research programs of the social sciences.

Many academic colleagues assisted us in this work. Dr. Lowell Brandner's critical reviews were of outstanding importance in revising the text of the argument. William Boyer, Don F. Hadwiger, Harold Jones, Robert McGinnis, Charles Eugene Ramsey, and Carl C. Taylor provided us with critical reviews or well-conceived comments which strengthened the argument or revived our spirits on the occasions when our confidence had flagged. Their efforts may not be discernible in the text but they contributed to the successful completion of the work.

Much of the empirical data was collected by student assistants. Those whose efforts substantially contributed to the completion of this work were: Charles Langford, Barbara Lanning, Mrs. Jean McDonald, and Charles Schilling. Finally, several typists were subjected to our time schedule and to the other demands authors make of them. Merrie Lou Douglas, Mrs. Kay Hodge, Mrs. Elizabeth Sendelbach,

Mrs. Norma Hartky, Mrs. Zoe Slinkman, and Mrs. Virginia Friesen performed well and patiently in typing successive versions and drafts of the manuscript.

Our indebtedness to the individuals named above is gratefully acknowledged but the responsibility for deficiencies of substance or interpretation that may be discovered rests solely with the authors.

WAYNE C. ROHRER
LOUIS H. DOUGLAS

Manhattan, Kansas
March 1967

CONTENTS

LIST OF TABLES

LIST OF FIGURES

1. THE AGRARIAN IDEOLOGY AND SOCIAL
   CHANGE   3
   THE TRANSITION OF AGRICULTURE   4
   IDEOLOGICAL EXPRESSION AND SOCIETY   11
   THE METHOD OF ANALYSIS   19

2. THE AGRARIAN TRADITION   25
   AGRARIANISM IN EARLY NATIONHOOD   28
   CLASSICAL AGRARIANISM IN THE PUBLIC
   ARENA   31
   AGRARIANISM IN THE PRIVATE ARENA   32
   AGRICULTURAL CHANGES IN AN
   INDUSTRIALIZING-URBANIZING SOCIETY   36
   NONTRADITIONAL BEHAVIOR: AMERICAN
   FARMERS ORGANIZE   41
   THE FORMATION OF AMELIORATIVE
   INSTITUTIONS   43

3. MODERN AGRICULTURE AND ORGANIZED
   RURAL LIFE   49
   AGRICULTURE IN THE MODERN ECONOMY:
   THE AMERICAN CASE   51
   FARM ORGANIZATIONS IN AN INDUSTRIALIZED
   ECONOMY   56
   THE ORGANIZED AND DIFFERENTIATED
   RURAL COMMUNITY   63
   HARVESTS OF MODERNIZATION AND ORGANIZATION   72

4. THE PUBLIC SECTOR OF RURAL LIFE 79
   RURAL PLURALISM 85
   THE STRUGGLE FOR REAPPORTIONMENT 90
   THE FEDERAL ARENA OF FARM POLITICS 95

5. SOCIAL CONTEXTS OF AMERICAN AGRICULTURE 105
   IDEOLOGICAL EXPRESSION IN KANSAS
   AND MASSACHUSETTS 107
   VIEWS TOWARD TWO VARIETIES OF PRESENT-DAY
   AGRICULTURE 121

6. CONCLUSIONS AND INTERPRETATIONS 141
   SOCIAL COSTS AND BENEFITS 143
   SYMBOLIC ANCHORAGES IN SOCIAL CHANGE 150
   CONTEMPORARY DECISIONS AND THE FUTURE
   OF RURAL AMERICA 157

7. FOREIGN ADVENTURES OF UNITED STATES AGRICULTURE 165
   FOREIGN TRADE IN FARM COMMODITIES
   AFTER WORLD WAR I 166
   WORLD WAR II AND ITS AFTERMATH 168
   FARM EXPORT MARKETS 171
   PUBLIC LAW 480 AND PROJECT ASSISTANCE 173
   PRIVATE FOUNDATIONS AND ORGANIZATIONS 176
   INTERNATIONAL ORGANIZATIONS 177
   THE RECIPIENT SYSTEMS 179

   SUMMARY 188

   INDEX 191

TABLES

Page

1. NUMBER OF RURAL FARM RESIDENTS EMPLOYED IN
BROAD INDUSTRY GROUPS, UNITED STATES, 1940-1960   50

2. POPULATION GAIN OR LOSS, 1950–1960, AS COMPARED
TO BUDGET INCREASE OR DECREASE, 1950–1960   88

3. WORKERS IN AGRICULTURE AND NONAGRICULTURE IN
THE UNITED STATES, 1880–1960   108

4. PERCENTAGE CHANGE IN THE NUMBER OF WORKERS IN
AGRICULTURE BETWEEN CENSUSES, 1880–1960   109

5. THEMES EXPRESSED IN SELECTED ARTICLES AND
ADDRESSES PUBLISHED IN ANNUAL REPORTS OF THE
STATE BOARD OF AGRICULTURE OF KANSAS
AND MASSACHUSETTS   111

6. DEMOGRAPHIC DATA FOR TWO AREAS OF
KANSAS   123

7. DATA FROM THE CENSUS OF AGRICULTURE FOR TWO
AREAS OF KANSAS   125

8. "IS MOVEMENT OF POPULATION AWAY FROM THE FARM
BASICALLY DESIRABLE OR UNDESIRABLE"   126

9. AGRARIAN EXPRESSION BY RESPONDENTS WHO HAD
DESIGNATED MOVEMENT AS UNDESIRABLE   128

10. AGRARIAN EXPRESSION BY RESPONDENTS WHO HAD
DESIGNATED MOVEMENT AS DESIRABLE   129

11. NUMERICAL CHANGE IN THE MALE RURAL FARM
POPULATION AND IN TWO AGE COHORTS, 1940–1960   133

12. NUMERICAL CHANGE IN THE MALE RURAL FARM
POPULATION AND IN TWO AGE COHORTS, 1940–1960,
UNITED STATES AND TWO SAMPLES OF COUNTIES   137

13.   INCIDENCE OF PART-RETIREMENT FARMING AMONG
FARM OPERATORS AGED 65 OR OLDER, UNITED STATES AND
TWO SAMPLES OF COUNTIES   139

FIGURES

I. CLEAVAGES IN AGRARIANISM: TRANSITION
VARIABLES IN PUBLIC AND PRIVATE SECTORS   81

II. TRADITIONAL AGRARIANISM AND MODERNIZATION
IN TWO SETS OF PUBLIC INSTITUTIONS   95

III. COUNTY OUTLINE MAP INDICATING SOUTHEASTERN
AND WESTERN AREAS OF KANSAS   122

THE AGRARIAN
TRANSITION
IN AMERICA

DUALISM
AND
CHANGE

1

THE AGRARIAN
IDEOLOGY
AND
SOCIAL CHANGE

Agrarianism is rooted deeply in the American experience.
Thomas Jefferson's articulation of the creed—the fundamental
nature of the agricultural industry, the societal benefit
derived from independent farmers, and the morally virtuous
quality attached to farming—made a sanctified calling of
agriculture. The secularly persisting ideology has provided
generations of lawmakers with an unassailable rationale,
indeed, a logic, for public programs designed to benefit
American farmers.

The deep roots have nourished a growth so vigorous that, with
the passage of time, agrarianism has transcended the bounds
of agriculture and has come to be applied to nonfarm
contexts. For example, the average American, in drawing a
correlation between urban residence and criminal activity,
attributes an inherent goodness to farm or rural living.
Agrarianism has some relevance in explaining the
suburbanite's penchant for a manicured lawn and for open play

3

spaces for his children. Furthermore, public officials have used
rationales derived from agrarianism to support programs of
urban renewal, city planning, or the rehabilitation of
juvenile delinquents.

Many of us acknowledge that if one is not currently residing
in bucolic surroundings, the next best status is to have been
a native of a rural place. A variation of this theme has been
expressed by occupants of or aspirants to the nation's loftiest
public position. Candidates for the presidency cite their
small-town or farm origins or their current connections to
these kinds of residences as eminently desirable biographical
features. Holders of the office of President have articulated
the need for national parks, wilderness preservation, and
highway beautification in phrases that would have
gratified Jefferson.

THE TRANSITION OF AGRICULTURE

At the outset this work was prompted by the persistence
of the agrarian ideology in a society that now has only a
minor fraction of its population engaged in farming. We were
impressed by the ease with which agrarianism was applied
in nonagricultural situations. Its persistence and the
wide uses to which it has been put suggest that agrarianism
is an American *idée fixe*.

The agrarian notion found fertile ground in America,
undoubtedly because farmers comprised a large proportion of
the total population. Agriculture exceeded nonagricultural
work as a source of employment for a century following
the Revolution. Rural residence predominated until World
War I. Rural and farm natives, born in America or
elsewhere, populated the burgeoning cities that accompanied
industrialization. The American transition from
rural-agricultural to urban-industrial was accomplished by
people acquainted with farming. Only within the last

generation has a substantial fraction of city dwellers been of urban birth.[1]

We may now raise a more specific question that gave impetus to this work. Will urbanized or metropolitanized people, many of whom have had neither a kin affiliation nor a nodding acquaintance with farming, willingly support the tradition of generosity toward agriculture? Stances taken on the legislative reapportionment issue bear on this question. Analyzing the skirmishing of contestants in this issue will provide some evidence. However, the consequences of reapportionment are still developing. As the major gains are made by suburban districts, the new constituencies influencing public policies may be more strongly oriented toward rural rather than urban norms. The new bottles of legislative representation may contain the old wine of agrarianism or at least a reasonable dilution thereof. Other sources—congressional testimony concerning farming and rural areas, for one—will yield cogent data.

The continuing quest for development in American agriculture has generated important practical problems. Successive disequilibriums were created by technological innovations; their accumulation brought about inevitable social adaptations. The political response, powered by the technology, often served to accentuate the disequilibrium within agriculture as well as between agriculture and the rising industrial economy.

This work concerns social change. One sort of change— economic development or industrialization—is an objective of people the world over.[2] Models of industrial development available to nations seeking change constitute, in several respects, extrapolations from the national ethos of industrialized countries. Whether the model provided is American, Chinese,

---

[1] Donald J. Bogue, *The Population of the United States* (Glencoe: Free Press, 1959), pp. 39–40.
[2] Clark Kerr et al., *Industrialism and Industrial Man* (Cambridge: Harvard University Press, 1960), esp. Ch. 1.

or Russian, the leaders who seek industrialization for their nations become implicated in programs whose rationales and methods were worked out elsewhere. Thus, American agrarianism is implicated in international affairs to the extent that our technical experts or diplomats hold it as a preferred form of agricultural practice.

Further, plans for national development now include ways and means of increasing agricultural productivity. Hence, advocates of industrial development recognize that achieving a successful transition requires a concurrent development of agriculture. It is no longer popular to ignore the farm sector, as was once the case.

Not only has agrarianism leapt the bounds of agriculture but it is reasonable to assume that the domestic ideology is carried abroad in the baggage of those Americans who represent us on foreign assignments. Our attention to this will be restricted to the formulation of concluding hypotheses.

Contemporary accounts of the course to industrialization—in China, eastern Europe, the Near East, Russia—suggest that farm distress and discomfort accompany the transition. The American rural dweller undergoing such transitions was and is caught between conflicting choices: either he perpetuates a hallucination, the good rural life inherited from his father's fathers, or he adopts the disappointingly unglamorous urban and industrial ways that cost his freedom. Fifty years after the one- or two-room country school was judged an anachronistic educational institution, consolidation of schools poses a hard choice in nonmetropolitan areas. Legislative reapportionment poses an even harder choice. Many Americans, resenting the Supreme Court's wrongheadedness in finding for equal representation of people, hold impeachment of its Chief Justice as their preeminent objective.[3] Some observers may categorize these

---

[3]Rural Democrats experience excruciating pain—a cost—on reapportionment. They often repudiate not only their party's majoritarian viewpoint on this issue but also the basic, even

behaviors as irrational and as not warranting serious
attention. However, understanding the rationales for seemingly
inexplicable behavior constitutes a leitmotiv for social
research. These illustrations show the costs of change
for certain segments of a population.
The American course to industrialization offers a recently
drafted and well-documented map of the route some nations
are taking or will take. We pose another question:
What empirical evidence of the transition to industrialization
is offered by analyses of the richly recorded American agrarian
expression? By analyzing published records of the American
experience, we shall obtain an accounting of the costs and
benefits farmers experienced in the transition.

We do not contend that the transition in other countries will
replicate the American course. Certain costs and benefits
realized here were dictated by conditions or institutions peculiar
to this country. However, certain circumstances will have
application beyond this nation's limits of culture, history,
or time. As a matter of fact, foreign agricultural technicians
in an emerging nation testify to the presence of a
generalizable fund of knowledge. Some tensions,
articulation of expressions, and group alliances would appear
to have cross-cultural applicability. These situations
will engage our attention.

Farm and rural populations declined proportionally as
industrialization and urbanization advanced in America.
Current plans of other nations assume these trends will
accompany economic development. It is patent that in a
society undergoing transition, farm or rural people
constitute its most numerous population segment during
much of the course of development. Yet, a society that

Jeffersonian concepts of the party itself. As one Kansas party stalwart
put it: "In the cities you have machines so you vote for whoever is
put up; in the country we vote for the man, not the party." What
this had to do with the issue is not clear. But it speaks eloquently
for the perpetuation of faith in Jefferson's chosen people.

has embarked on the transition places a higher value on improvements in the nonfarm sectors. The American course commenced in a milieu predominated by farmers who followed a sanctified calling. The granting of high esteem to nonagricultural occupations eroded the eminence of farming. The downward shift of the locus of agriculture in the national economy of nineteenth-century America partially accounted for the expression of farm distress and discomfort in industrialization.

We believe that viewing the transition from the vantage point of bystanders to the process will provide insights unobtainable from other viewpoints.[4] This suggests another dimension of this work—the hope that our analyses will contribute to the understanding of ways of reducing the discomfort of contemporary farm people, domestic or foreign, who experience the transition. The sheer number of people included in the farm population of any nation now engaged in industrialization recommends that we contribute evidence that may diminish future discomfort. It is possible that the agricultural problem of the U.S.S.R. is based in the public policy that preferred industrial development to development of the farm sector. The Russian incentive system apparently has been attuned to urban-industrial performance rather than to agricultural achievement.

It is insufficient to argue that because industrialization is such a popular panacea it is therefore irresistible and irrevocable and that, as a consequence, farm people are powerless to express alternatives. Even the most despotic regimes, including

[4]William McCord, *The Springtime of Freedom* (New York: Oxford University Press, 1965); David Apter, *Ideology and Discontent* (New York: Macmillian–Free Press, 1964); Paul E. Sigmund, *The Ideologies of the Developing Nations* (New York: Frederick A. Praeger, 1963). These sources rely to a great extent on views expressed by the "agents" of development, the national political figures who articulate policy. On the other hand, Daniel Lerner with Lucille W. Pevsner, *The Passing of Traditional Society* (New York: Free Press, 1964), used an approach that corresponds more closely to ours.

the Nazis, have been required to account to public opinion.
In other words, it is unlikely that farmers will be
required to submit passively to victimization.

However, in clarifying the options available to farm people
it will be well to note that whether or not farmers are
to accept technology and urbanization does not constitute
a valid option. Maps of strip cities and the censuses
unequivocally document the urban increase in America.
A nation bent on industrialization will concomitantly
experience increasing population density in some areas.
Moreover, American farmers epitomize to the world that the
reward of increased agricultural production accrues to those
who accept technology. Farmers who choose to oppose
urban and industrial expansion *per se* would exercise the
Luddite option.

Choices that farmers may exercise include a range of
adjustments that are consistent with a productive agriculture
and concurrently an industrializing economy. Choices
illuminated by our analyses will be presented at the conclusion.
Because agriculture in the modern economy is implicated
with other sectors, options available to farmers will emanate
not from agriculture alone but from its systemic implications
with other sectors as well. Therefore, among the views
utilized will be some from nonfarmers. By recourse to these
data we can more fully explicate agriculture in its
societal context.

If we can understand agrarianism as this nation changed
from a distribution of isolated, independent villages to
a large-scale system including relatively few high-density
concentrations of interdependent, interrelated locales, and as
the economy evolved from one in which most worked the soil
to a situation in which fewer than one of ten do so, then we
shall learn some details of the maintenance of stability in
the midst of social change. Agrarianism retained its viability
through nearly two centuries of history. Its generalization to
nonfarm situations and its perseverance label it a hardy
human artifact.

The latter rationale is relevant to our study for two general reasons. First, the transition will not require the length of time in other nations that was required here; changes that transpired over generations in America will be telescoped into decades elsewhere. Thus, although time constituted a resource conducive to adjustment in this country, it appears as though time will serve as a constraint in the nations more recently embarked on the transition. When time is in short supply, not only are missteps more critical but tensions of the transition are heightened. Second, the persevering of the agrarian ideology promises to yield empirical evidence useful in another context. Many social scientists avow that modern man requires anchorages similar to those that his forebears enjoyed. These observers note that the ritual and tradition of the homogeneous village, environs that constituted the social settings for our immediate ancestors, were stabilizing factors that gave life a social meaning. They also observe that the contemporary urban industrial community has not developed institutions or traditions fulfilling the social needs of a heterogeneous population. American agrarianism appears to constitute a suitable vehicle for testing the validity and efficacy of this observation.

Agrarianism constitutes a suitable vehicle because of its persistence and wide application. Given these characteristics, however, we wonder as to what extent it has only "lip service" recognition from certain status groups or social aggregates within America and, on the other hand, to what extent it has a binding quality.[5] Otherwise stated: When is agrarianism a ceremonial form that constitutes a manifest expression of some latent socially important concern and when does it constitute a substantive, nonfictional ideology?

---

[5]Robin M. Williams, *American Society: A Sociological Interpretation*, 2nd rev. ed. (New York: Alfred A. Knopf, 1960). Williams' section on "Cultural Fictions" was useful in this statement.

IDEOLOGICAL EXPRESSION AND SOCIETY

Ideology expresses social views which represent, ostensibly or otherwise, those in whose interest they are stated. The expression includes not only a view of the world as it is but preferences as to the sort of world that ought to be. Further, ideology includes not only the self-appraisal of societal values but also the valuational aspects of any series of instrumental arrangements and their manipulation for the purpose of achieving a preferred distribution of resources or values. To the extent that ideologies consist of expressions in evaluative terms of goals and systems, their content may lack descriptive accuracy. Ideology provides one of the means by which the uncomfortable "is" (the facts of life) may be made a bit more livable. Mannheim has alluded to this in defining ideologies as "more or less conscious disguises of the real nature of the situation."[6]

Observers of ideology—historians, philosophers, political scientists, social psychologists, sociologists—provide us with two analytically distinct questions that structure this study. The first: What relationships exist between ideology and the society in which it is observed? The answer to this question may be stated in static terms. Alfred von Martin portrayed the Renaissance as a transitional era in which the commercial ideology of the rising merchant class countered the feudal ideology.[7] Ideologies were specified to host groups in a population. The ideological contestants may be viewed at a single point in time. However, "contestants," following Selznick,[8] may through mediation become allies, and in the bargain modify ideological stances to suit the alliance. Units of observation in this kind of research may be the ideological

---

[6]Karl Mannheim, *Ideology and Utopia* (New York: Harcourt, Brace and Co., 1954), p. 49.
[7]Alfred von Martin, *Sociology of the Renaissance*, trans. W. L. Luetkens (New York: Harper and Row, 1963), pp. 5–9.
[8]Philip Selznick, *TVA and the Grass Roots* (Berkeley: University of California Press, 1949). Selznick's argument specifies the way in which an ideological position becomes rearticulated to suit local

contestants, the social composition of the ideologically disposed, or the nature of the arrangements worked out between contestants.

The second question—How does ideology persist?—concerns the interrelationship between the ideological system and the society or groups to which it attaches over time. A persisting social form attributes a dynamic dimension to the analysis. Specifying these questions led to a conceptual understanding, explicit in the ordering of these questions, which provides the scheme of approach to the problem at hand.

Two sociologists, Bell and Lipset, argue persuasively in separate works that ideology has ended as an effective force in Western societies.[9] For example, the Welfare State has been accepted by those formerly antagonistic to its imposition and program. At the same time, adherents of the left have essentially ended their attacks on private enterprise and capitalism by ceasing to push for nationalization of industry or other important segments of the economy. In essence, observed consensus cuts the ground from under once viable ideological stances.

The Bell and Lipset conception of ideology is that intellectuals expound and communicate it. Ideology tends to be relevant to and located in the political institution of industrializing societies. Hence the emerging nations, those seeking industrial development, constitute the contemporary loci of ideological discourse. Masses of men react to this discourse and are motivated to act. However, in this view, the viability of ideology lessens as industrialization advances. Ideological

---

circumstances. A strong commitment to the "grass roots" doctrine held by federal government personnel was modified in the context of local arrangements. Local organizations that became affiliated with the public program represented only one segment of the grass roots. In order for the TVA to enter local areas legitimately, it was unnecessary to implicate the entire spectrum of local organizations and institutions.

[9]Daniel Bell, *The End of Ideology* (Glencoe: Free Press, 1960), p. 373; S. M. Lipset, *Political Man* (Garden City: Doubleday-Anchor, 1963), Chapter 13, "The End of Ideology?"

stances become incorporated into policy, and ideology ceases
to be required.

So far as Bell and Lipset are concerned the nineteenth century
constituted an ideological cauldron in the West. With the
advent and fuller development of industrialization, Lipset
notes, ideology has come to be articulated by sociology.
Apparently, a social science discipline will provide the forum
in which competing ideas joust; the outcome of this contest
will be the conceptualization of symbols which will serve to
motivate men in the complex society.

We hold that Bell and Lipset deal with only certain ideologies
that have withstood a test of time. Assuming longevity to be
the criterion of success, these were the successful cases, the
persisting expressions. The identified ideologies around which
Western intellectuals no longer collect are perhaps no longer
causes. It is our contention that such varied stances as
protest, the status quo, or justifying a social stratum's position
constitute sufficient bases for articulating an ideology. When the
observer acts to delimit units of observation, he places some
unpopular ideologies beyond his ken. However, the large-scale
industrialized, mass society includes ideological expressions
"in waiting." An appropriate turn of events—for example, the
control of the Republican party in the United States since
1961 by ultras, resulting in the formulation of themes that
many observers had relegated to the ideological cemetery—
may resurrect and render viable themes which many
intellectuals had regarded as beyond recall. Bell and Lipset
do not accord their ideological articulation with an audience
in the contemporary world. We argue that the intellectuals
who could motivate specified segments of the population—
whether they are inarticulate by nature, or articulate but
currently out of political favor—confront a problematic
situation; perhaps their expression is still to be articulated,
or having been articulated, is in the process of acquiring
adherents.

Perhaps the amount of publicity about an ideology has an
inverse relationship to the extent of actuality of the ideology

in social life. For example, the development of what may
roughly be called a welfare society has been accompanied
by a sharp rise in the number of ultra-right-wing publications
and radio programs. This appears to be an accurate delineation
of the contemporary American scene. Conversely, during the
application of the principles of Social Darwinism in the 1880's
and 90's an unusually large amount of the literature of Utopian
Socialism was published. Moreover and finally, it cannot be
maintained that consensus destroys ideology because ideology
constitutes consensus. Perhaps the consensus within retains
viability as it is countered from outside. It would appear that
labor and management representatives may agree for years
or a decade but that this consensus may be dissipated by
changes in environment. In other words, consensus may be
temporary.

Consider the following illustrations. If we view indigenous
American Utopian experiments of the nineteenth century that
did not persist—for example, New Harmony, Brooke Farm,
the Shakers—we designate them as lost causes. But had these
communities enlarged their compass of advocates and persisted
to contemporary times, American society would be differently
arranged. Because they died aborning, their relevance is very
much like that which many people attach to archaeological
artifacts: interesting, quaint, fascinating, but largely irrelevant
for many tasks of today. In addition, let us refer to a recent
lost cause—technocracy. Had technocracy achieved a wide
following, America would today have a different social milieu.

These belief systems remain available to us in extant literature.
Undoubtedly, some intellectuals are attempting to determine
why these causes were lost and how their programs might
have been modified or might be reshaped to render them
successful in this world. If viable, cogent themes are abstracted
from past ventures these themes would fuel social movements.
Adherents of these social movements would agree on the
worthwhileness of themes, programs, or rationales that were
newly enunciated or drawn from the existing reservoir of
ideological expressions. We cannot realistically state that

"ideology has ended." Nor can we seriously query: "The
End of Ideology?"

Therefore, ideologies like other social forms are initiated,
persist, become transformed, and might die. A persisting
ideology, for example, agrarianism, provides an empirical test
whereby interconnections with social groups and the content
or form of the ideological expression may be secularly observed.
Observing the procession of groups or aggregates that have
affiliated with an ideology will allow us to demonstrate the
use made of the ideological expression. Hofstadter demonstrated
that an ideological system—Social Darwinism—attached to
different segments of the population at different times and
that the rationales for this expression were quite different
between the nineteenth and twentieth centuries.[10]

This discourse would now posit the view that widespread social
support for a specific ideology may end but that ideological
expression does not necessarily do so. The ideology may be
"dormant."[11] The 1964 presidential election manifested clear
ideological stances to a much greater extent than had been
the case for nearly two decades. The argumentative may
counter that a presidential campaign provides a short-run
ideological expression. Perhaps so. Perhaps a viable ideology
requires competing counterexpression in order to persist. Or,
perhaps a viable unopposed ideology requires a substantial
popular base of support to persist. Or, perhaps an ideology no
longer viable in one social segment becomes reinterpreted and
translated to apply in an area of life which contemporaneously
provides fertile ground. For example, contemporary American
Protestantism includes adherents to the social action orientation

[10]Richard Hofstadter, *Social Darwinism in American Thought*, rev. ed.
(Boston: Beacon Press, 1955).
[11]Rolf Schulze, "The Recession of Ideology?" *Sociological Quarterly*,
5, no. 2 (1964), 148-56. Schulze's view, that ideological expression
recedes rather than dies, corresponds to our notion of dormancy. Our
thesis agrees with Schulze's.
Reinhard Bendix, "The Age of Ideology: Persistent and Changing,"
in David Apter, *Ideology and Discontent* (New York: Free Press,
1964). Bendix' view in this regard and several others supports
the views we have taken.

and advocates of the individual salvation orientation. It is not at all obscure to trace the interrelatedness between advocates of these modes of belief and ideological allies found in other institutional structures. Humanitarianism versus rugged individualism, the Welfare State versus the "least government is the best government," and the environment versus heredity dialogues constitute paired alternatives from other frames of reference that readily complement expressions articulated in the religious contexts. The advocates of these themes apparently have little difficulty in translating theological preferences into preferential positions in economic, political, or social contexts.

That ideology is conceptualized and communicated by intellectuals appears to be valid. Literate expression that motivates others would be the intellectual's forte. What concerns us more, though, is that agrarianism, which was articulated by Jefferson and Taylor, who qualify as intellectuals, has contemporary importance.

A persisting ideology may be disaffiliated from one context and affiliated to another. Social Darwinism, which involved a translation of the Darwinian thesis into social terms, was rendered intellectually sterile as an explanatory thesis of social change. Scientists and intellectuals marshalled evidence which empirically refuted this version of the thesis. But Hofstadter documented its persistence. He indicated how it became viable and suitable in advocating American imperialism and racism.[12] One is reminded of the lyric, "The song is ended, but the melody lingers on." An intellectual articulates and specifies an ideology, but its credibility lies outside the intellectual province. In fact, its rationale may have disappeared but the belief system continues. Apparently the belief system remains credible so long as it constitutes a basis for action for some elements in the society.

Bell's question—"But how long can a myth sustain, when the reality constantly belies it?"—has been partially answered by

---

[12]Hofstadter, *Social Darwinism,* especially Chapter 8.

Hofstadter. A long time.[13] Festinger, Riecken, and Schachter
provide empirical evidence of stubborn allegiance to a belief
system which had been unequivocally disconfirmed.[14] They
observed a group of "believers" who predicted the world's
inundation. The believers would escape the watery grave in
being transported by flying saucer to another planet, where
they were to be trained to return to a habitable earth as its
colonists. The flood did not occur. Some defections followed
disconfirmation. But some remained loyal to the belief system
despite its being discredited. The loyal remained faithful to
the same ideas they had held in the days prior to the predicted
flood. Perhaps man's inventiveness, vis-à-vis ideological content,
is essentially unbounded; certainly in this instance, our abilities
to rationalize a continuing attachment to a belief system
demonstrate a sort of inventiveness.

The Festinger, Riecken, Schachter study also provides
additional observations useful to the present argument. The
believers' idea system embraced a bundle of beliefs and
practices. For example, complementary beliefs in extrasensory
perception, dianetics, flying saucers, and reincarnation held
esteemed places in their belief system. A bundle of beliefs
served as a reservoir from which an alternative vehicle could
be chosen when a specific item was rendered unattractive. For
the leftist who no longer seeks nationalization of the domestic
economy it is reasonable that he translate this grander objective
into a less grand one. Perhaps he now seeks government
participation in the economy by the construction and operation
of "yardstick enterprises." Thus a government-owned steel plant
would be sufficient and suitable in contemporary terms instead
of government ownership of the steel industry. Surely
intellectuals of the left, center, and right have a reservoir of
alternatives to be proposed when appropriate. These alternative
or subsidiary ideologies would be viable if their expression

---

[13]*Ibid.*, p. 271
[14]Leon Festinger, Henry W. Riecken, and Stanley Schachter, *When Prophecy Fails* (Minneapolis: University of Minnesota Press, 1956).

mobilized people. An ideological system that motivates others has neither ended nor died.

Moreover, it may be contended that the ideas, practices, and belief system of the "believers" who were observed by Festinger *et al.* constituted their version of reality. To others their belief system was the sheerest kind of nonsense, but adherents were motivated to expend time, money, and effort in preparing for the flood. Disconfirmation occurred just once, and thus it did not "constantly belie" reality. But it was unequivocal. If "disconfirm" be accepted as a rough synonym for "belie," we have a refutation of Bell's rhetorical question.

An essay by Miller aids us to determine whose version of reality is articulated. In his critique of the self-fulfilling prophecy, Merton's elaboration of the thesis that the definition of the situation constitutes the real situation, Miller concludes by classifying Merton's work as a provocative hypothesis.[15] Miller's reappraisal considers the question: Whose version of reality concerns us? The participants' or the observer's version? For example, Merton demonstrates in his work that a belief is father to the act.[16] Hence, the notion that ideology serves to motivate action is implicit in the Mertonian view. In his illustration of the Last National Bank the self-fulfilling prophecy serves as a short-run belief system with outstanding relevance and cogence. The possible translation of inaccurate beliefs into reality was remedied, in the hypothetical example, by corrective action. By the organization of a federal insurance program, whereby depositors were assured that their money was safely held by a member bank, the necessity to participate in a "run on the bank" was rendered obsolete.

But the notion that the self-fulfilling prophecy was false is no more valid than was the depositors' view that the poor condition of the Last National Bank was true. Miller argues that

---

[15]Cecil Miller, "The Self-Fulfilling Prophecy: A Reappraisal," *Ethics,* LXXII, no. 1 (1961), 46–51.
[16]Robert K. Merton, *Social Theory and Social Structure,* rev. ed. (Glencoe: Free Press, 1957), Chapter 11.

truthfulness or falsity, in a predictive sense, is beyond our grasp at this point in the social sciences, because these sciences are developmental rather than cumulative. Hypotheses whose truthfulness or falsity can be demonstrated are restricted to the physical sciences and mathematics. Miller observes that the view that the inaccurate action was in fact inaccurate was a construct in the thought processes of the observer. It was not necessarily in the thinking of participants. Intellectual constructs are not necessarily compatible with the social environment in which an action is observed. On the other hand, when an ideologue's expressions are socially accepted the intellectual's expression of reality coheres with some social segment's view of reality.

THE METHOD OF ANALYSIS

Our conceptual need was for a model which would allow ideology to serve as a source of and as a constraint on change. This recalls Mannheim's observation that change may be "progressive" or "regressive."[17]

Because our work concerns change, some social change generalizations have importance. Moore cited evidence of the accelerated rate of change and of the increasing incidence of planned change. He observed, following others, that the inconsistency or poor fit between the ideal and the actual tends to produce change.[18] Moore also noted that the modern nation which includes diverse and discordant elements harbors sources of change within its structure. This constitutes a rationale for the study of agrarianism in an industrializing society. The agricultural segment in an industrializing society may be subjected to discriminatory or favorable policies in the industrializing process.

---

[17]Karl Mannheim, *Ideology and Utopia;* Mannheim associated "ideology" with regressive and "utopia" with progressive change.
[18]Wilbert E. Moore, *Social Change* (Englewood Cliffs: Prentice-Hall, 1963), pp. 66–68.

Moreover, Moore noted that the transition to industrialization has been viewed in its consequences for elements of the society "but only rarely is attention given to the interaction of structures in juxtaposition."[19] Observing the interaction between agriculture and other segments of American society will enlarge our understanding of the process of industralization. By viewing agrarian expression over time as articulated by farmers or their advocates, we will be able to specify change or nonchange in the order of expression and the relationship between an expression and response. Furthermore, when agrarian expression is viewed as it was articulated by advocates who were near to or distant from American urban industrial centers, enhanced knowledge of structural responses will be obtained.

Our method also is indebted to Levinson's observation that monolithic societies—either nonliterate communities or "encysted subcultures within modern nations"—display a uniformity of ideology.[20] America has evolved within several generations from an essentially monolithic situation in which agrarianism was the cogent ideology. The American course to industrialization has been recently run and is well recorded. How fared agriculture in this evolving environment? And how fares agriculture in an industrialized urbanized society?

George Herbert Mead's thesis of *The Philosophy of the Present* has substantial relevance for change and for our elaboration of ideological expression.[21] Mead stated that the present emerges out of the past. And, correspondingly, the future emerges out of the present. In the introduction to the collected essays written by Mead, it is stated that past and present are irreversibly linked but that the present "is not completely determined by

---

[19]*Ibid.,* p. 106.
[20]Daniel Levinson, "Idea Systems in the Individual and Society," in George K. Zollschan and Walter Hirsch, *Explorations in Social Change* (New York: Houghton-Mifflin Co., 1964), p. 313.
[21]George H. Mead, *The Philosophy of the Present* (Chicago: Open Court Publishing Co., 1932).

the past out of which it arose."[22] There is always something
novel or abrupt in the present. Furthermore, the fact that a
problem has been identified constitutes a means of
distinguishing between the present and past. An analysis of
American agrarianism will identify watershed events, those
occurrences that distinguished between epochs.

Applying Mead's thesis to our problem, we would posit that
men frequently seek solutions to current issues by reference to
solutions tested in the past. The designation per se of a
problem and its exposition are likely to render the whole
matter in ideological terms. Preferred views of the world are
articulated as a problem is designated. Moreover, present
arrangements and a new view of them serve as alternative ways
to regard the past. In other words, conceptualizing the present
along Meadian lines suggests a reinterpretation of the past.[23]

Our argument notes that a surviving form—agrarianism—has
contemporary cogence and relevance. The relationship between
agrarianism and its contemporary social structures exceeds
our interest in the mere persistence of ideological expression.
One might ask by inference from Mead's thesis: What
consequences, indeed, misadventures, accrue to a diversified,
heterogeneous society undergoing rapid change, if its ideologues
look to the past for solutions to its problems? Do social diversity
and rapid change render some proposed solutions inoperable?
Applied social science research serves one pragmatic purpose
in this kind of society: to narrow the lag between problem
delineation and proposals for amelioration. This does not cast
the applied scientist as *the* ideologist. He would be one among
many ideologists. Our analysis of agrarianism will shed light
on these questions.

Our method is rendered in the following context: The
heterogeneous society will have a variety of problems; the
variety per se may immobilize or confuse decision-making in

---

[22]*Ibid.,* introduction by Arthur E. Murphy, p. xvii.
[23]Recent reinterpretations by historians of the Reconstruction Era
in the American polity serve as a contemporary illustration.

public or private sectors; the variety will cause different segments to define the past and present differently; preferred future arrangements will vary among segments; finally, several proposals may be followed concomitantly.

Secondarily, this study concerns persistence of an ideological form. Festinger, Riecken, and Schachter observed an empirical instance of unequivocal disconfirmation of the occurrence of a prophesied cataclysm. In searching the literature on Messianic movements they had discovered that unequivocal disconfirmation did not weaken some adherents' advocacy of a belief system. In the instance they observed, some members rejected the group and the belief system following disconfirmation. Others, faithful believers, on the other hand, became short-run proselyters following disconfirmation. Seeking additional believers was a departure from the way they had behaved in the period preceding the date of the anticipated flood. The authors indicate that proselyting was a means of dignifying the belief system; that is, after disconfirmation, recruiting adherents rendered the belief system tenable to those who had retained their faith. Each recruit confirmed the veracity of the beliefs retained by members who resisted disconfirmation.[24]

The matter of disconfirmation of a belief system has relevance for persistence and change in ideology. For example, unequivocal disconfirmation may be insufficient to lessen attachment to ideological positions. If this is so, the marshalling of facts will not disabuse people of beliefs they hold. An ideological system may be tenaciously held after its empirical justification has dissipated. Hence, neither persistence nor change manifests a "rational" correlation between ideology and society. Persisting agrarianism in industrializing America allows us to observe an ideology that secularly experienced a diminishing proportional population base. One might observe that agrarianism ought to have died.

---

[24]Festinger, Riecken, and Schachter, *When Prophecy Fails,* Chapter 7, pp. 193–215.

However, disconfirmation is not likely to be comfort-inducing over the long run. Undoubtedly, some evidence contradictory to one's preferences is rationalized or ignored. Furthermore, if it concerns a politically organized segment of the population numbering millions of people, like the American farm population, it seems unlikely that those who experience disconfirmation will suffer stoically. Moreover, in an interdependent economy, many nonfarm people will be affected who are not numbered in the specific category.

Our data include expressions of ideology as these were broadcast across a period of time. We will be able to specify changes in expression if these occurred. Our empirical data include historical and contemporary evidence. Analysis of addresses to delegates included in the annual reports of two State Boards of Agriculture, congressional hearings on federal programs to serve rural people, empirical evidence collected from sample populations with various relationships to farming concerning their attitudes toward migration of people from farm areas, and views expressed by observers regarding legislative reapportionment will explicate varied expressions of agrarianism through time and the group attachments of its advocates or opponents.

This analysis observes interaction of the urban industrial segment of society with the rural and agricultural. At least some aggregates of people within the nonfarm segment— agricultural teachers and researchers, agriculturally related business men, and persons related by kin ties to farmers—have a more than incidental interest in American farming. So it is that while this book concerns farmers, it is not exclusively about farming. The agrarian ideology concerns more Americans than those who espouse it in their self-interest. In this regard, agrarianism is analogous to the civil rights movement that concerns more Americans than those who directly espouse or oppose its actions. Agrarianism as a persisting ideology provides us with a highly visible vehicle to discern connections between idea systems and social arrangements.

2

THE
AGRARIAN
TRADITION

The origins of the rural orientation of American life are
both eminently respectable and persuasively practical. The
values of a system free from the well-known ills of the
industrial city of eighteenth-century England and France were
early laid down by Thomas Jefferson as rules for the good
society. The class of free agriculturists pursuing the husbandry
of plants and animals and applying the best science available
to the land, constituted indeed, "the chosen people of God,
if ever he had a chosen people."

In the most comprehensive statement of his beliefs regarding
political economy, Jefferson left a heavy imprint on the
structure of American values:

Corruption of morals in the mass of cultivators is a phenomenon
of which no age nor nation has furnished an example. It is
the mark set on those, who not looking up to heaven, to
their own soil and industry, as does the husbandman, for
their subsistence, depend for it on casualties and caprice of

customers. Dependence begets subservience and venality,
suffocates the germ of virtue, and prepares fit tools for the
designs of ambition. This, the natural progress and consequence
of the arts, has sometimes perhaps been retarded by accidental
circumstances: but, generally speaking the proportion which
the aggregate of the other classes of citizens bears in any state
to that of its husbandmen, is the proportion of its unsound
to its healthy parts, and is a good enough barometer whereby
to measure its degree of corruption. . . . The mobs of great
cities add just so much to the support of pure government
as sores do to the strength of the human body.[1]

Though Jefferson lived to revise his views about the benefits
and the desirability of commerce and industry, he had already
struck a responsive note that touched off one of the major
continuing themes in American ideology—rural life contained
the best of American culture; its evils were concentrated in the
cities. From the very first establishment of the Republic to
the present, political leaders have rallied to the cause of
preserving the best of American character by attending to the
well-being of rural life. Typically, public policy has been
generous to agriculture; parallel programs for city welfare
have been comparatively neglected.[2] Civic, church, and
educational leaders have, often subconsciously, perpetuated a
substantial rural ingredient in the Great American Dream.

It was suggested above that in addition to the stimulus given
by Jefferson and those who articulated, in a form increasingly
exaggerated, the rural virtues, there were dominant and
driving social forces in support of American agrarianism. First
of all, it was an agrarian society that was forming, first as
British colonies, later as an isolated, frontier republic. The
ownership of land was widespread, highly prized, and easily
achieved. Cities were small and few in number. New York,
the largest metropolis, had a population of 33,000 (Manhattan

---

[1]Thomas Jefferson, *Notes on Virginia,* cited in Alpheus T. Mason,
Free Government in the Making (New York: Oxford University
Press, 1949), p. 359.
[2]This sentence is written with full awareness that it is threatened with
early obsolescence. It is the impending storm that the agrarian value
now faces that has motivated this writing.

Borough) in 1790; Philadelphia 28,500; Boston a little more than 18,000. To say "American" was synonymous with saying "farmer."

As the frontier was pushed westward during the nineteenth century, from the Appalachians to the Rockies, the agrarian features of American culture changed, but they did not become less prominent. As the urban features became more pronounced, they, too, were impressed with many rural characteristics. In fact, Sjoberg cited the preindustrial city as remarkably similar to the rural village.[3] For example, this city form and the village were isolated units. The city's economy, like the village's, was based on animate power, handicrafts, and a price system set by bargaining. A social organization articulated through kinship relationships and emphasizing superordination by males, the elderly, and a local elite provided order and control.

One could infer that the earliest cities formed in America constituted agglomerations of several villages. Industrialization changed the city form from rural-like arrangements. But these industrialized cities have remained subservient to rural-dominated state governments and have been populated, in large, by migrants from farms or villages. By inference, we conjecture along two lines: The legislatures inhibited the provision of the kinds of specialized services required by densely settled populations; urban populations were inarticulate in expressing their urbanistic requirements or sought village-like arrangements in the urban setting.

So long as cities were village-like and isolated, rural rationales for economic, political, and social behavior approached adequacy. The corporation, the centralized urban political party organization, the world market, and the large-scale organization of specialized talents to provide mass-produced and mass-distributed goods and services were accompaniments to the transition from the preindustrial to the industrialized state.

---

[3]Gideon Sjoberg, "The Pre-Industrial City," *American Journal of Sociology*, 60 (March 1955), 438-45.

Our attention now turns to American agrarianism and farming as this urban-industrial trend accelerated.

AGRARIANISM IN EARLY NATIONHOOD

When the United States of America was a century old, the number of persons employed in manufacturing exceeded the number in farming. Moreover, farmers have become a minor fraction of the labor force during the century which commenced with the Civil War. Through one-half of our history as a nation and during the entire colonial period farming was known in practically every household. Even so, the agricultural basis for our economy, polity, and society was being eroded years ago. How did farmers and their advocates view this change? The positions taken, the expressed views of the world were founded in Jeffersonian conceptualization.

The agrarian ideology served as the American rural social creed, according to Johnstone.[4] The first of the trinity of propositions specified that the farmer was independent. Self-sufficiency was not only possible but necessary for the isolated American farm family; the sale of produce allowed this family to purchase necessities that were not home-produced. The independent man was not only the equal of any other man, the independent farmer literally was in partnership with God. Farming was an organic whole, a gestalt; it was not readily rendered in a means-ends context.

The second point of agrarianism was that agriculture is the basic industry: "agricultural fundamentalism." Nonfarm occupations or populations relied on the farmer for their sustenance. In essence, the nonfarmer's prosperity was farm-based. Contemporary observers who state that an agriculturally based depression leads to a general depression articulate this view.

---

[4]Paul H. Johnstone, "Old Ideals versus New Ideas in Farm Life," *Farmers in a Changing World: Yearbook of Agriculture, 1940* (Washington: U. S. Government Printing Office, 1940), p. 117.

To designate agriculture as the basic industry was reasonable in nineteenth-century America. At least three-fourths of the population farmed. Some undoubtedly regard present-day expressions of agricultural fundamentalism anachronistic; however, this expression retains cogence. A Kansas farmer whose land was to be taken by the expansion of a military installation warned readers of a small city newspaper that if the taking of farm land for nonagricultural purposes continued, "there will be no bacon and eggs on the breakfast table."[5] The letter-writer—his expression could be multiplied by similar views from millions of Americans—simply had not conceived of America without a sufficient domestic agriculture.

The third point in the trinity, that agricultural life was natural and good, was the most important according to Johnstone. This involved a corollary: urban life was neither natural nor good. Generalizing from this to specific characteristics, spokesmen held that commercialism, frillish affectations, uncalloused hands, or too great attention to comfort or leisure corrupted man and sapped his virtue and morality. Farmers followed a sanctified calling.

Colonial and nineteenth-century America provided land of low initial cost to millions who had known land hunger. Available farmland constituted perhaps the strongest magnet attracting immigrants to this country. Moreover, land ownership constituted access to esteemed statuses: in some instances the right to vote was restricted to land owners. The institution of private property, preempting land to freeholders, the high esteem attached to land ownership, conjoined with the agrarian ideology, developed an awesome, massive force in American society.

Another merging of belief systems occurred in the formative years of the American Republic. The virtues of democracy and agrarianism were intertwined. Although Griswold wrote that

---

[5]"The Readers Say This," *Manhattan Mercury* (Manhattan, Kansas, April 15, 1964).

urban people are more effective than rural in stimulating democratic growth, his thesis has not noticeably affected the myth-system.[6] Jefferson's concept of agrarian democracy may have been somewhat illusory. But his prodigious faith in "those who labor in the soil," his praise of rural society, and his unflagging devotion to improving agricultural practices combined to provide the momentum that has given agrarianism powers of survival.

Agrarianism did not derive its strength only as an agent of democracy. Rural virtues constituted the standard for assessing human endeavors. Jefferson looked for an enlightened, public-spirited, wholesome Man and found him in the sturdy yeomen of the piedmont and the Appalachians. Jefferson proposed a governmental order overly representative of these men, and advocated minimal policies sufficient for their governing. He lived to question his dream for American society. Finally, he resolved one principle; that of change and adjustment to change, which was circumscribed by the exception "nothing then is unchangeable but the inherent and unalienable rights of man."

The numerical superiority of agriculturists had a special significance in a democracy. The weight of the rural proportion of the citizenry made the moral precepts of agrarianism mighty. Jefferson was not defending a minority right in upholding the agrarian interest; he was energizing the majority. He temporarily routed an opposition that gave credence to a limited and indirect democracy. Perhaps Jefferson would have restated his democratic thesis on other than agrarian grounds in his later days.

The alliance of agrarianism with democracy powerfully supported rural people regardless of the frailty of the concept when subjected to critical analysis or to the forces of history.[7] Griswold was able to show clearly and finally that urban rather than rural areas fed democracy and that farmers

---

[6] A. Whitney Griswold, *Farming and Democracy* (New York: Harcourt, Brace and Co., 1948); see especially the concluding chapter.
[7] Grant McConnell, *The Decline of Agrarian Democracy* (Berkeley: University of California Press, 1953), is a most valuable critical study of agrarian democracy.

demonstrated their affection for democracy in peculiar fashion.[8]
The institutions of the American countryside included the
small local government, homestead ownership, country school
and church, individually owned small businesses, and a spirit of
equalitarianism. These spelled democracy to the farmer.

CLASSICAL AGRARIANISM IN THE PUBLIC ARENA

The view of government set forth by classical agrarians has
received insufficient emphasis. These views exhibit an amazing
hardiness, an ability to endure in the most hostile environment.
The canons of government asserted by agrarians are basic to
the good society. Canon one, it has been suggested, is that
least government is the best government. Large, energetic
government could be corrupted by "aristocracies of interest"
that would exploit the rest of the nation.[9] Widely distributing
the powers of government would prevent the concentration of
power. When federal power was used to protect agriculture this
antipathy to central government was expediently accommodated
to the exigencies of ameliorating the lot of farm people. In
the formative years, the targets of resistance were the protective
tariff and the Bank of the United States; the main weapon
was the Constitution as interpreted.

A second canon posed by John Taylor was that the states were
sovereign. This canon expressly limited the powers of the
federal government. The tariff legislation advantaged the few
and consequently was detrimental to the nation and particularly
to farming. The Bank charter granted monetary policy making
to the aristocracy; agrarians noted that those who govern money
govern all. The miniscule federal government of 1810 was
apprehensively viewed by John Taylor. Contemporary distrust
of central government was mirrored in his remarks:

Turn your eyes toward a government accoutred in the complete
panoply of fleets, armies, banks, funding systems, pensions,

[8]Griswold, *Farming and Democracy*, pp. 179–82.
[9]John Taylor, *Construction Construed and Constitutions Vindicated*
(Richmond: Shepherd and Pollard, 1820), pp. 11–18.

bounties, corporations, exclusive privileges; and, in short,
possessing an absolute power to distribute property, according
to the pleasure, the pride, the interest, and the avarice of
its administrators; and consider whether such a government
is the servant or the master of the nation.[10]

Equality was the third canon of government the agrarian
democrats held. Taylor articulated a complex argument as he
found it necessary to exclude the Negro from the scope of
equality. However, his antagonists, the Federalists, who
championed the ascendant bankers and merchants, were
portrayed as anti-egalitarian. They were parasites quick to
use the federal government against the people. Their designs
could be prevented by the widest dispersion of power. Private
power was preferable to governmental and local was
preferable to centralized power.

The most significant unit of government in the Jeffersonian
usage was the "ward." The ward corresponded to the township.
Individual participation was practical and effective in the
ward's affairs. The functions of the wards were to be expansive,
including those essential for peace, good order, educating the
young, and progress. The impact of technology on this local
unit has constituted a trial of the contemporary agrarian.

AGRARIANISM IN THE PRIVATE ARENA

A large segment of the agrarian's life was devoted to the free
exercise of his talents. The individual wealth-producer in the
context of freedom of contract and small property ownership
required an enlightened yeomanry. Hence, schools followed
closely on the occupancy of virgin land.

Taylor particularly emphasized the importance of equality of
the private individual as well as the public citizen. Widespread
ownership of small farms, a requisite of the good society,
recognized the power that inhered in property. Excluding
Negroes from the doctrine of equality rendered possible a

---

[10]*Ibid.*

plantation economy. However, the *minifundia* rather than the *latifundia* should be emphasized.

The Physiocrats' doctrines that land was the source of all wealth, that tillers and miners ("farmers and mechanics") constituted the productive class, that trading and financial interests were "parasites," were adopted by Taylor. He believed that producers were continually exploited by the parasites and were held in permanent subjugation and exploitation.

Whereas Jefferson favored a natural aristocracy that would be replenished by a system for elevating and training the most able, Taylor opposed aristocratic notions in principle; but his laissez-faire penchant coupled with his disposition toward equality (for Caucasians) would work toward the same outcome. Both champions of classical agrarianism had agreed on the value of laissez faire. However, Jefferson shifted toward the end of his life and conceded that the great social principle was change. Only "the inherent and inalienable rights of man" were exempted from the principle's operation.

The American Republic's growth nullified Jefferson's aspirations. Changing conditions dictated an adapting ideology, and to some degree Jeffersonian agrarianism became obsolete. However, the norms of the ideology have persisted. This persistence has occasioned a struggle between the situation and the ideal, between the existing and the preferred order.

Evolving agrarianism discarded some standards—devotion to laissez faire and equality—as it incorporated new norms— organization of farmers into pressure groups and farmers' rapprochement with businessmen rather than with laborers— which indicated shifts in values and expectations of farmers. Recently, the concept of agri-business manifested further shifts in political power and in the relationship between farmer and businessman. Additional capital and land required by the technological revolution altered the position of farmers in undreamed-of ways.

However, the norms of Jefferson were not significantly outmoded before the opening of the twentieth century.

Although the ethical simplicity of the Jeffersonian democracy
was not readily incorporated into the rural way of life,
still it was venerated and applied with relatively little
inconvenience. Thus, small local governments continued past
their usefulness; distrust of central government remained part
of the farmers' creed; the commerce of cities continued to
be regarded as the servant of agricultural production.

Agrarianism emphasized local self-sufficiency. Subsistence
farming was to be elevated to better and higher standards of
living. Home production, processing, and manufacturing assured
independence from the "parasitic class"—the merchants,
manufacturers, and bankers. That which could not be produced
locally was imported; it was hoped that imports and locally
produced surpluses would balance. This manageable traffic
need not disturb the happy enterprise or stability of the local
community, nor threaten its population's self-determination.

Self-sufficiency was prized as farmers moved toward the Pacific.
Settlements began on a subsistence agricultural base. Westward
from the Mississippi, however, subsistence became translated
into survival. Great Plains agriculture not only extracted a
heavy toll but its conditions dictated more complex means of
reaching the good life. The complexities have not diminished.

Before Jefferson's death, American agriculture had entered into
a market economy. Ingenious men exploited the resources of
mid-America and other regions. New visions of how to make
money superseded the glamour of the self-sufficient small
holding or plantation. The sturdy yeoman no longer was
invited, as John Taylor of Caroline had been, to serve in the
United States Senate. Leadership went to men who held
another view of the destiny of American society. The words
of Hammond are illustrative:

Liberty became transformed into *laissez-faire*. A violent,
aggressive, economic individualism became established. The
democracy became greedy, intolerant, imperialistic, and
lawless. It opened economic advantages to those who had
not previously had them; yet it allowed wealth to be
concentrated in new hands only somewhat more numerous

than before, less responsible, and less disciplined. There were unenterprising thousands who missed entirely the economic opportunities with which America was thick.[11]

Leadership in a national context fell to the lot of businessmen and industrialists in America. The aspirations of Jefferson and Taylor were rendered anachronistic with the commencement of urbanization and industrialization.

No one today speaks for a nation of suburbanites as Jefferson spoke for a nation of farmers. The metropolis as a haven for democracy and as the fountain of cultural development has had no single articulate advocate. In fact, the city's case may be articulated by those that want to render it in a peasant village-like form—Frank Lloyd Wright—or those who want to marry the best of the city with the best of the country— Christopher Tunnard—or those who want to create forms— Victor Gruen—that elaborate the city's unique requirements in view of its unique qualities.[12] Perhaps the American ideologies of the next decades will be those that advocate means of living our lives in the urban setting.

As industrialization advanced, ideological questions had to do with proper or better ways to achieve its ends. Means could be public or private or could involve a blending of public and private. The economy that has become industrialized, however, confronts problems of consumption and distribution which exceed the attention devoted to problems or methods of production. Its focus of attention shifts and in the shifting a new ideological base is illuminated. But although agriculture was being transformed, farmers and their articulate advocates continued to express agrarianism by reference to circumstances that had existed in the past.

---

[11]Bray Hammond, *Banks and Politics in America from the Revolution to the Civil War* (Princeton: Princeton University Press, 1957), p. 327.
[12]David R. Weimer, *City and Country in America* (New York: Appleton-Century-Crofts, 1962); see relevant sections of Chapters 7 and 8.

AGRICULTURAL CHANGES IN AN URBANIZING-INDUSTRIALIZING
SOCIETY

As the agriculturist became a part of a business economy his
environment changed. The virtue of independence had been
rugged individualism. The prizes of the competitive struggle
went to those with the sharpest prehensile claws; in this arena
farmers had some advantages and some disadvantages. At any
rate, by 1870, commercial farmers had become "inextricably
enmeshed within the exchange nexus, their standard of living
dependent upon railroad concerns and eastern wholesale-
manufacturers. . . ."[13] Interdependence with urbanites has
been the lot of the American farmer for more than a century.
Two particular advantages were available to farmers in adapting
to the changing social and economic order. One was the
numerical majority held by rural people in the total population.
This condition assured to them a predominant voice in elections,
particularly in local jurisdictions, and made it certain that
agrarian interests would not be overlooked. The second
advantage was the persistent theme of classical agrarianism
which was absorbed by many urban residents irrespective of
their nativity. This attitude persists to the present.[14]

On the other hand, farmers were disadvantaged in terms of
sheer economic striving. The corporation's shelter behind the
guarantees to individuals in the Fourteenth Amendment
rendered the struggle unequal.[15] Freight rates, warehouse and
commission charges, and prices received were beyond the
farmers' control. The harvest of farm production, being subject
to weather vagaries, exposed farmers to natural caprice in

---

[13]Howard R. Smith, *Government and Business: A Study in Economic
Evolution* (New York: Ronald Press, 1958), p. 123.
[14]At a conference of a major party in one of the farm states, an effort
to endorse reapportionment in its platform was rebuffed with the
assertion that rural voters had better skill than city voters in
selection of legislators as well as better material to choose from.
[15]The first Supreme Court opinion holding that the word "persons"
as used in the Fourteenth Amendment to the Constitution included
corporations is found in *Santa Clara County v. Southern Pacific
Railway*, 118 U.S. 394 (1886). It has been a continuing dictum of the
Court since this decision, notwithstanding occasional minority dissent.

addition to human caprice. The nineteenth century accentuated the individual farmer's struggle with a loss of social esteem and idyllic contentment. The rugged demands of farm life— and these were not imaginary in the days before the Rural Electrification Administration, tractors, and paved roads— were translated into a sign of rural superiority.

While rugged individualism was the dominant theme of frontier-agrarianism, a minor theme of collectivism must be noted. Perhaps Turner overly stressed the former in his frontier thesis of American history.[16] As de Tocqueville noted, however, the frontier made collective effort indispensable. One writer has suggested that the "frontier American did not hesitate to carry the principle of logrolling and house-raising . . . the vigilantes committee and cattle raisers' association, into politics."[17] He termed this "empirical collectivism." Cooperative effort was mingled with individual action, and the farmer learned well that the instrument of government was his most effective agency of cooperative action.

Outlines of agricultural fundamentalism had become clarified by the close of the nineteenth century. It had been firmly established in the social structure of numerous American institutions. Agricultural fundamentalism had acquired attributes needed for the times and added another vital strand to our agrarian ideology. Rural values were strengthened to withstand the onslaught of urbanization. Jeffersonian idealism had not been discarded but had been supplemented.

Agriculture was proclaimed the base necessary for the development of the arts, commerce, and industry. Though it was believed that rural dwellers could live without cities, the obverse did not hold; "do away with the produce of our farms, and grass will grow in every main street in America." Thus did a candidate for the presidency in this century touch

---

[16]Frederick Jackson Turner, *The Frontier in American History* (New York: Henry Holt and Co., 1920).
[17]Currin V. Shields, "The American Tradition of Empirical Collectivism," *American Political Science Review,* 46 (March 1952), 107.

a responsive sentiment among the citizenry. More sophisticated was a comment of one of the nation's acknowledged business leaders of the 1920's as he asserted: "Agriculture is the greatest and fundamentally the most important of our American industries. The cities are but the branches of the tree of national life, the roots of which go deeply into the land. We all flourish or decline with the farmer."[18] Agriculture constituted the American wellspring.

Furthermore, the countryside had been the predominant source of supply of people for the cities. This cityward migration has been viewed with considerable approval. With appropriate opportunities for nonfarm employment, "particularly if it is nearby, the healthy flow from farm to city takes place, and that is probably a reason why statistics show farm productivity and living levels are highest in the vicinity of urban centers."[19] The nearby city aided farmers to obtain a good level of living. But the city benefited from receiving rural or farm natives.

The farm-to-city migration commenced in the first half of the nineteenth century. Johnstone noted that while farm youth were encouraged to enter farming and were exhorted to be successes, nevertheless the models provided to Americans as exemplars for their lives and vocations, even models specified by farm periodicals, stressed not the traditional farm values but those of the commercial world. Success was defined by commercial acumen. Migration contributed to urban growth and created markets for farmers. No longer was farm produce bartered in the nearby market. A railroad carried produce to the distant, growing cities. In addition, American agriculture afforded goods for export. Agricultural exports purchased goods from Europe or provided financial returns on investments which foreigners had made in our developing economy. World

[18]Bernard Baruch, quoted in D. Gale Johnson, "Government and Agriculture: Is Agriculture a Special Case?" in John H. Bunzel (ed.), *Issues of Public Policy* (Englewood Cliffs: Prentice-Hall, 1964), p. 170.
[19]Willis R. Knight, "Agriculture," in Walter Adams (ed.), *The Structure of American Industry* (New York: Macmillan, 1961), p. 9.

War I was the approximate turning point in that America
became a creditor rather than a debtor nation.[20]

Farmers produced specialties for the market. No longer was it
suitable to weave, to cobble and to manufacture at home the array
of goods produced by the independent farmer. The farmer
purchased goods that formerly cost him labor added to materials
which came from his holding. In short, farmers became
businessmen—producers of goods for sale and purchasers of
consumption goods.

Those farmers that organized to seek improvement took on other
urban behaviors. For example, Johnstone pointed out that when
farmers determined that business was unyielding in its demand
for tariff protection, they sought equivalent protection for
agriculture. Farmers' cooperatives, a collective business method,
incorporated the financial practices of existing commercial
organizations. Cooperatives accepted procedures which only
recently farmers had maligned. During the latter years of the
century farm management practices were urged on farmers. The
land-grant colleges encouraged this "rational" business procedure
which had been stated earlier in the farm press. Johnstone
notes how a committee of agricultural leaders which met in
1926 allocated typical farming costs to the operator's salary,
return on investment, depreciation, and so on. Johnstone
continues:

The idea that the farm is an investment on which the farmer
should expect to draw interest above and beyond the direct
reward for his labor or that the farmer should make a monetary
calculation of the value of his labor is an application of
principles entirely harmonious with the modern commercial
world of the city and industry, but it is a radical departure
from the older agrarianism. The emphasis upon a paper
concept of ownership, as opposed to a use concept, is obvious;
and the remoteness from earlier attitudes which identified the
farm as a home providing an opportunity for the production
of the necessities of life by the sweat of the brow, where

---

[20]Arthur P. Chew, "The Meaning of Foreign Trade for Agriculture,"
Farmers in a Changing World: Yearbook of Agriculture, 1940,
pp. 571–73.

obstacles were natural rather than social, can hardly be
exaggerated.[21]
For an ideology to make sense to the farmer depicted by
Johnstone it had to depart from classical agrarianism.

The technological revolution in agriculture, which got under
way in the nineteenth century, and the business revolution,
which overlapped the nineteenth and twentieth centuries,
massively eroded agrarianism. By your own action if you were
to use machines built in Moline or Detroit and if you were to
use a farm management system devised by the state college of
agriculture or by a management service, you cut the ground
from under the notion that agriculture was the basic industry.
Traditional agrarianism was rendered clayfooted for those
farmers who entered an agricultural system designed for
providing goods to an industrial economy.

Although we specified farm and rural people as bystanders to
industrialization, they were drastically affected by the transition.
Many sent their grown children to urban industry. Moreover,
economic, political, and social currents originating outside rural
communities and, in fact, emanating from the transition,
impinged on their styles of life. As a matter of fact, American
farmers were so affected that they and their advocates provided
us with an extensive written record of farmers' attitudes,
impressions, and biases founded in the change.

Their views on farming and rural life and on the city and
industry, their lobbying for legislative or executive action, their
political programs, the numerous conferences reported in farm
and urban media, constitute a rich record. Nonfarm advocates
of agrarian views included agricultural colleges, state and
federal departments of agriculture, general farm organizations,
cooperatives, and commodity organizations. While the richness
of the record provides a fruitful harvest, it also requires the
exercising of parsimony. So we have restricted our attention
to expressions of agrarianism.

[21]Johnstone, "Old Ideals versus New Ideas," p. 144.

Reapers, plows, planters, and binders were mechanical devices
that became available to farmers in the nineteenth century.
These allowed individual farmers to produce more crops than
they previously had with given amounts of labor. New forms
of transportation, new ideas about soil fertility, and 'new
marketing or processing methods, were initiated in this era.
Each helped to change farming. Farm journals and state boards
of agriculture were started between 1800 and 1850. Agricultural
educational objectives were enunciated for the newly organized
fairs, agricultural institutes, and neighborhood discussion
groups. More than the addition of agricultural machinery was
involved in changing American agriculture; a spectrum of
actions yielded change and improvement.

NONTRADITIONAL BEHAVIOR: AMERICAN FARMERS ORGANIZE

Carl Taylor documented the details and consequences of the
American farmers' movement between the Civil War and
World War I.[22] The Grange, the Farmers Alliances, the
Agricultural Wheel, Populism, the Farmers Union, the Equity
movements, and the Farm Bureau rocketed forth in this half-
century. They fought business but became businessmen in this
era. Farmers were seeking, and they sought in the company
of others.

Farmers' organizations emulated and countered organized efforts
of the remainder of society. Farm organizations sought political
intervention to control middlemen and railroads, to confront
problems of agricultural markets, prices, and credit. Qualifications
for membership in a farmers' organization were discussed at
the initial—1872—meeting of the Kansas Board of Agriculture.
Whether membership ought to be limited to farmers in a
secret, grange-like organization or open to any well-wishers was
an issue. One speaker feared that an open organization would

---

[22]Carl C. Taylor, *The American Farmers' Movement: 1620–1920*
(New York: American Book Co., 1953). Taylor devotes 14 of a total
of 20 chapters to the organized activities of farmers in the
inter-war period. For the student of American agrarianism the
Taylor work is required reading.

be "unacceptable . . . since outsiders can come in and run . . ."
the organization.[23] The published remarks did not elaborate
on what sorts of people qualified as "outsiders." Positive and
negative criticism was directed toward the Grange. The end
was not discussed but the means were: they knew they
wanted to organize.

The Farmers Cooperative Association, the organization initiated
in Kansas in 1872, designated that membership was to be
limited to farmers or those "practically interested in farming."
A somewhat exclusive character was followed. Perhaps the
"somewhat exclusive" character manifested practicability. For
example, the composition of an organizing meeting held ten
years earlier, which had been intended to form a similar
organization, is reported to have included eleven Kansas
farmers among the 200 dues payers.[24]

It appears that some farmers were not motivated to join in
representing their occupation in the industrializing economy
of the latter half of the nineteenth century. This must have
been distressing to those who wanted to organize. Many farmers,
moreover, must have been discouraged by the irony that
nonfarmers joined but farmers did not. Apparently two
different anchorages were evolving for farmers. First, those
prone to organize regarded an interest group as a basis for
organization. Second were those farmers who manifested little
or no interest in organized efforts. The kinds of farmers related
differently to the agrarian ideology. As a matter of fact, the
first farmer had almost no personal investment in two of the
three points of agrarianism. He did not regard farming as an
occupation of independent enterprisers who followed the good
life. Those who saw no need for organization probably held a
commitment to classical agrarianism. Attachment to or
detachment from classical agrarianism appears to have been
symptomatic of an evolving differentiated farm community.

[23]Kansas State Board of Agriculture, *Annual Report of 1872* (Topeka:
State Printing Office, 1873), p. 34.
[24]I. D. Graham, "The Kansas State Board of Agriculture,"
Kansas Historical Collections, Vol. 17 (1928), p. 788.

Those who relinquished their attachment to agrarianism may have modified their definition of the good life from an agricultural base to a base in the rural community. Those who resisted organization, by inference therefrom, held fast to their independence. Perhaps an illusory independence was their sole harvest from the promised trinity.

Organized efforts of American farmers undoubtedly affected the harvest realized in the political arena. Edwards indicated that while farmers stridently advocated their interests, they did not achieve a rich harvest in legislative or executive action.[25] Government actions following the Civil War were more consistent with nonfarm commercial or industrial interests. The Populist party exceeded its degree of success in 1892 by a greater success in 1894. Success was short-lived, however. The 1896 election outcome signaled the demise of farmers' parties in national politics, according to Edwards. Thereafter, their electoral successes were restricted to jurisdictions below the national constituency. These political movements of the latter years of the century were farmer-led. However, the decline of Populism apparently coincided with the general disappearance of farmers from elective political positions. On balance, perhaps the real consequences of the farmer political ventures of this era were acquisitions of some governmental services.

THE FORMATION OF AMELIORATIVE INSTITUTIONS

During the last four decades of the nineteenth century policies were effected that supported agrarianism. The Homestead Act, 1862, intended to place freeholders on land they were to operate. Land grants to railroad companies were to open lands for settlement. Land grants subsidized the companies but it was intended that the assurance of populated districts adjacent to the rights of way would encourage the construction of roads. The United States Department of Agriculture was formed as

---

[25]Everett E. Edwards, "American Agriculture: The First 300 Years," *Farmers in a Changing World: Yearbook of Agriculture, 1940*, pp. 263–65.

an independent agency in 1862, and was granted cabinet status in 1889. This was the first instance wherein an occupational segment received representation in the federal executive branch.

The land-grant colleges (1862), the experiment stations (1887), and the cooperative extension services (1914) constituted a complex in innovation which originated in the nineteenth and carried over into the new century. Each followed its predecessor by roughly a human generation and each had a small-scale prototype. It appears that as one element in the complex became established, it indicated a need for a further extension which had not been implemented within the earlier element.

Some federal programs consistent with farm organization demands appeared in the last fifteen years of the nineteenth century and several new programs were instituted in the early years of this century. The Sherman Antitrust Act, the Interstate Commerce Commission, rural free delivery, postal savings, and the Federal Reserve Bank were farm-organization inspired.

The expression of dissatisfaction channeled through farm organizations obtained indemnification from federal programs. It was recognized that most of the problems confronting farmers were national or at least interstate, and thus the federal government was the ameliorative agency. State agencies—the State Boards of Agriculture in Kansas and Massachusetts— apparently constituted protest organizations. Annual meetings were forums devoted to discussion of farm problems. The sovereign states may well have been immobilized by the regional nature of agriculture's problems on the one hand, and by the agrarian's localistic orientation to problem solution on the other.

Rural America was no longer a serious competitive alternative as compared with urban industrial America. Taylor observed that by the close of the nineteenth century land ownership no longer yielded its holder the social eminence and political prestige which was accorded to those engaged in other pursuits.[26]

---

[26]Taylor, *The American Farmers' Movement,* pp. 284-86.

A shift in occupational eminence involved a downward move for farmers. Further, the nation's free land had disappeared. Free land had been a magnet for immigrants and for farm-reared natives and had resulted in increased rural population. By 1910 or thereabouts, it had perhaps become apparent that only one or none of a farmer's children would follow his occupation. This factor may have been made evident because of the rapid acceptance of machinery into farming operations by 1910.[27]

Toward the close of the nineteenth century, farmers' dissatisfaction, manifested by Populism and other actions, was widespread. Pessimism replaced optimism, which had been based on the ease with which farmland, a sufficient and rewarding end in and of itself, had been sought and obtained. Land no longer conferred esteemed social status·as it had in earlier America. And finally, nonfarm occupations, especially those in commerce and industry, were more esteemed than were agrarian callings.

In the half-century 1860–1910, apparently it had become appropriate for external institutions to defend and promote farm and rural life. It was no longer sufficient to render rural conditions equal to urban; the federal government, state governments, and the agricultural colleges were to support rural life.
Social trends—the United States became more urban than rural in this century's second decade—alarmed groups concerned with rural America. President Roosevelt's Country Life Commission, which reported in 1909, was preoccupied with social trends affecting rural life.

The report perhaps climaxed the nineteenth-century chorus. It sought a renovation of rural life. Mixed feelings greeted its publication. Johnstone observed that the Commission remained

---

[27]Alvin S. Tostlebee, *The Growth of Physical Capital in Agriculture, 1870–1950* (New York: National Bureau of Economic Research, 1954), p. 65.

an executive activity; it never received congressional sanction.[28] Also, he noted that so far as many farmers were concerned the commission was supported by do-good city dwellers and failed to deal with production problems. Sanction of the clergy, educators, and government officials was not matched in its reception by farm audiences.

Seven men composed the Commission: two represented land-grant colleges, two represented the mass media—one a farm journal and the other a magazine with a general audience appeal—one was a United States Department of Agriculture official, one represented a farm organization, and the seventh remains unidentified except by name. The latter two were named after the original five commissioners had been designated. The identifiable person of the latter appointments was the commissioner most closely allied with farmers. His appointment was an afterthought. How ironic, in view of Jefferson's idealization of the farmer as representing God's chosen occupation, that nonfarmers received the initial appointments to this commission of inquiry. A century after Jefferson's observation, the farmer was not the most qualified to guide an inquiry concerning farm conditions.

The report articulated agricultural fundamentalism while noting the deficiencies of rural life. Deficient social conditions were: the poorly organized rural society, a lack of knowledge of agricultural conditions and potentialities, poor educational systems, farmlands held by absentee owners or for speculative purposes, the lack of good highways, the mean life of farm women, and others. The deficiencies would be mitigated by an extension service, agricultural surveys, highways and parcel post, and investigations of the marketing system. The independent farmer, who was identified in the report as "the separate man" or "the unattached man," had come to symbolize a problem rather than a state to be envied.[29]

---

[28]Johnstone, "Old Ideals versus New Ideas," p. 154.
[29]"Report of the Country Life Commission," *Public Document No. 705*, U.S. Senate (Washington: U.S. Government Printing Office, 1909).

Institutions external to farming implemented the report. Even more, implementation through the federal government received a positive rationale from the report. Extension and perhaps vocational agricultural programs were inspired by the report; a survey of European farm credit institutions may have been generated by its conclusions; Galpin credited the Commission with instigating rural sociology as an area of academic work.[30]

The College of Agriculture, University of Wisconsin, sponsored conferences from 1911 to 1914 having to do with country life.[31] Occupations of the 61 speakers at three of these conferences are available to us. One-half, 31, were educators (19) or clergymen (12); farmers or farm leaders ranked third in incidence with 11 speakers; bankers, editors, and politicians were other occupational categories represented. Farmers were involved. But the country life problem was delineated by persons other than farm residents. This suggests that the initiation of the country life movement had the best interests of the rural community at heart but that the heart of the rural community was not included in the movement. Apparently, conceptions of rural life and problems varied by the kind of relationship one had to agriculture.

The period between the Civil War and World War I witnessed the shift from a substantially agricultural to a largely industrialized economy in the United States of America. Until World War I Americans were farmers by residence or by sympathy and sentiment.

---

[30]Josiah Galpin, "Rural Sociology," *Bulletin No. 37* (U.S. Office of Education, 1924), pp. 45–52.
[31]*Reports*, Wisconsin Country Life Commission Meetings of 1911–1914 (Madison: College of Agriculture, 1915).

3

MODERN
AGRICULTURE
AND
ORGANIZED
RURAL LIFE

Some years ago Davis observed that agriculture required a minor fraction of the labor force in industrial nations.[1] Australia, New Zealand, and Denmark, which had notable agricultural economies, featured modern manufacturing sectors as well. The modern industrial economy correlates with an efficient and modern agriculture. In such an economy, agriculture and industry are not antagonists.

In fact, evidence that nonfarm and farm occupations blend well may be obtained from analyzing the occupational characteristics of the farm population of the United States of America. (See Table 1.) Change in the number employed in the several industrial groups also indicates that agriculture and mining

---

[1]Kingsley Davis, "Demographic Foundations of National Power," in Morrow Berger, Theodore Abel, and Charles H. Page (eds.), *Freedom and Control in Modern Society* (New York: Van Nostrand, 1954), pp. 224–27.

TABLE 1.   NUMBER OF RURAL FARM RESIDENTS EMPLOYED IN
BROAD INDUSTRY GROUPS, UNITED STATES, 1940–1960*

Industry Group	Decennial Census			Percent 1960 is of 1940
	1960	1950	1940	
Total employed	4,673,002	7,974,046	9,616,046	48.6
Agriculture, forestry, and fisheries	2,821,750	5,662,812	7,560,986	37.3
Mining	32,225	104,489	111,114	29.0
Construction	174,474	246,749	191,905	90.9
Manufacturing	561,573	747,010	579,033	97.0
Transportation, communication, & public utilities	114,533	164,720	134,070	85.4
Wholesale & retail trade	321,282	346,638	278,162	115.5
Finance, insurance, business, & repair services	79,903	100,553	74,924	106.6
Personal, entertainment, recreational services	140,077	148,161	294,776	47.5
Professional, related services	241,141	212,538	243,111	99.2
Public administration	89,239	94,588	70,911	125.8
Industry classification not reported	96,805			

*SOURCE: *Census of Population* for each year: 1940, Vol. II,
Table 18, p. 48; 1950, Vol. II, Table 55, p. 102; 1960,
PC (1) 1C, Table 91, p. 221.

experienced the greatest declines between 1940 and 1960. Fewer
rural farm residents of the future, will, if recent trends persist,
be engaged in agriculture than in nonfarm occupations.
Whereas in 1940 almost eight out of ten in the rural farm
population were engaged in agriculture, by 1960 only six out
of ten followed farming. Perhaps the industrialized economy not
only enhances production efficiencies in agriculture but
provides nonfarm employment opportunities for those who
prefer farm living.

While farming declines in its fraction of the labor force, and
farmers decline to a minority numerical position, they still

wield political power. Hadwiger indicated that middlewestern office seekers avidly wooed farm voters because they voted more variably than did nonfarmers.[2] An avidly wooed electorate looms large to legislators who have been successful. Hadwiger noted that although the farm bloc has declined as a monolithic power center because the evolving heterogeneity of agriculture correlated with a disunited agriculture, farm organizations have obtained recent concessions and have successfully pressed their interests. American farmers utilize the political institutions of a modern economy in sophisticated ways.

AGRICULTURE IN THE MODERN ECONOMY:
THE AMERICAN CASE

As the agricultural segment drifts toward a minor position in its national economy, it ceases being independent and self-sufficient and becomes implicated with the industrial sector. As Kerr *et al.* state the nature of the interdependence, "The silent night of pre-industrial society yields to the insistent requirements of continuous operations."[3] Nature dictated the daily and annual tempo of life and work in the traditional rural community. Interdependence shunts aside nature as the sole agent determining the farming round. In a symbolic but telling way the annual controversy between rural and urban people over Daylight Saving Time illustrates the dispute as to who sets the schedule.

Interdependence between rural and urban seems to increase as the transition unfolds. Ducoff indicated that some of the interdependence may come about through conjoining farm and nonfarm occupations in a single household.[4] Moreover,

---

[2]Don F. Hadwiger, "Political Aspects of Changes in the Farm Labor Force," Center for Agricultural and Economic Adjustment, *Labor Mobility and Population in Agriculture* (Ames: Iowa State University Press, 1961), pp. 50–72.
[3]Clark Kerr *et al., Industrialism and Industrial Man* (Cambridge: Harvard University Press, 1960), p. 38.
[4]Louis J. Ducoff, "Occupations and Levels of Living," *A Place to Live: Yearbook of Agriculture, 1963* (Washington: U.S. Government Printing Office, 1963), pp. 19–25.

occupations from the two segments may be conjoined in an individual's work pattern. For example, in 1959 nearly one-quarter (23.7 percent) of all farm operators worked off their farm 200 days or more.[5] The percentage had approximately quadrupled since 1929. Distinctions between rural and urban blur for individuals who work in each area.

The rural-urban fringe intermixes residences of farm and nonfarm families. Distinctions that rested on a basis of no interaction between farm and city people are modified. Nelson, observing the similarity between city and country styles of life, cited an apparent diminution of differences in attitudes and value systems.[6] In this respect Hadwiger's conclusion, based on a comparison of the voting records of rural and urban congressmen, that there are still discernible rural and urban viewpoints is probably a sufficient constraining observation: Differences have lessened but some distinctions remain between city and country.[7]

Urban and industrial ideas penetrate rural areas in ways other than those specified. For example, Firey cites the readiness with which farmers in the High Plains of Texas responded to threats that state or federal government would control their access to underground water supplies.[8] They used an urban-type response to the threat, namely, the coalition of special-interest groups. As the threat subsided, the coalition broke apart. In traditional rural communities organizations were not used this way. The nontraditional rural community borrows an organizational form that has been widely used by urban people.

---

[5]*U. S. Census of Agriculture,* 1959, Vol. II (Washington: U.S. Department of Commerce, 1960), p. 113.

[6]Lowry Nelson, "Rural Life in a Mass-Industrial Society," *Rural Sociology,* 22, No. 1 (1957), 20.

[7]Hadwiger, "Political Aspects of Changes," pp. 63–67. For a hypothesis as to the "real" distinction, Chapter 4 of this text notes that representatives from areas of economic growth vary substantially from representatives of areas experiencing economic decline.

[8]Walter Firey, "Coalition and Schism in a Regional Conservation Program," *Human Organization,* 15, No. 4 (1957), 17–20.

Raup observed that farmers will be served by fewer but larger service centers.[9] He inferred that the evolving centers will be attractive to organizers of labor unions, that unions will be formed in closer proximity to farmers than heretofore, and that with proximity will come exposure to unions and the knowledge that farmers share common problems with wage workers.

Other effects of interdependence may be noted. An industrialized economy will produce farm machinery along with other manufactured goods. Hence a nation that has an industrialized modern economy will be likely to have a mechanized agriculture. The effects of the mechanization of agriculture have been so well documented that a mere listing is sufficient: As farmers mechanize, they enlarge the acreage operated, reduce labor requirements, and increase capital investment and use of credit. In a certain sense, these changes within agriculture may be said to have been caused exogeneously.

Another effect of industrialization on the agricultural sector was suggested by Ruttan.[10] Through much of our history, development in agriculture preceded development in the nonfarm sector. It appears as though this sequence may have been more characteristic of the North and East than of the South. Therefore it may have been an artifact of the nonnational basis of our economy during the last century. However, Ruttan assigns the leading role in development to nonfarm sectors of the present economy.

Our evidence that present-day agriculture is implicated with the society and economy in different ways includes four items. The changing balance is manifested in that a decline in the power position of farmers has been underway; internally, agriculture is undergoing such drastic change that the industry

---

[9]Philip M. Raup, "Economic Aspects of Population Decline in Rural Communities," Center for Agricultural and Economic Adjustment, *Labor Mobility and Population in Agriculture* (Ames: Iowa State University Press, 1961), pp. 95–106.
[10]Vernon W. Ruttan, "Agriculture in the National Economy," *A Place to Live*, pp. 135-38.

confronts a new epoch. These changes indicate that a
redefinition of agriculture will render agrarianism inapplicable.
Another credible option is that we will unabashedly collate
agrarianism with the aggregate of people involved in farming.
This collation may be awkward but it would not be the first
time that contradictory social behaviors have been married.

The Demographic Position of Agriculture

The farmers and farm managers category of employed persons
ranked ninth of ten categories in the *1960 Census of
Population*.[11] If farmers, farm managers, farm laborers, and
farm foremen are aggregated, then farming ranks eighth of nine
employed categories. Additional pertinent features have already
been described. One context designates the rural farm population
as a minor category: the nonwhite population in 1960
outnumbered farm residents and this disparity will increase.
Thus the component of population that has been designated
as the minority group will in the years ahead be substantially
larger than the farm population.

United States Supreme Court's Ruling on Reapportionment

The 1962 rulings whereby urban residents were judged to be
underrepresented under existing state plans for legislative
representation is a new posture. In fact, the 1962 decisions
reversed a rule established by the Supreme Court fifteen years
earlier regarding congressional apportionment.

The relative decline in the power position of farming has
quantitative and qualitative dimensions. The demographic data
indicate that farmers are not independent by self-definition,
nor may agriculture be designated the basic industry; the
Supreme Court ruling contests the view that they are more
virtuous than other populations. These changes render
agrarianism an anachronism.

---

[11]U.S. Bureau of Census, *U.S. Census of Population: 1960,
General Social and Economic Characteristics, U.S. Summary*
(Washington: U.S. Government Printing Office, 1962),
Table 87, p. 216.

The remaining two trends specify the changing nature of agriculture.

Vertical Integration in Agricultural Production

The application of industrial procedures to livestock production introduced economies of scale, established different credit arrangements, and rearranged the farmer's relationship to the agricultural enterprise. A question posed by integration: where does management rest?[12]

The Agribusiness Concept

Some that have used this concept indicated that 40 percent of the economy lay in the agribusiness sector.[13] Wholly disregarding the validity of this conceptualization—is it valid to aggregate food sales and distribution enterprises with farm production enterprises?—the notion is ingenuous in that it collected domestic enterprises. In other words, domestic distribution and processing segments could handle foreign farm production.

On the one hand, vertical integration disputed notions of an inherent difference between agriculture and other industrial enterprises. Farming had no unusual virtues as contrasted with other occupations: the farmer is no closer to the Deity than is the follower of another vocation. On the other hand, the agribusiness concept enlarged the compass of agriculturally related enterprises. While joining several segments of the economy may have had political relevance, the aggregation diminished the agricultural fraction. Changes in farming have involved adjustments by the farm population to the new economic environment. Combining farm and nonfarm occupations and incorporating nonhousehold members into farm

---

[12]Louis Ploch, "Social and Family Characteristics of Maine Contract Broiler Growers," Bulletin 596 (Maine Agricultural Experiment Station, 1960), p. 38.
[13]John H. Davis and Ray A. Goldberg, *A Concept of Agribusiness* (Boston: Harvard University Graduate School of Business Administration, 1957), p. 8.

management have altered the nature of the farm enterprise.
Concepts articulated outside of agriculture—the "one man, one
vote" decision of the U.S. Supreme Court and the agribusiness
notion of agricultural economics—constituted impingements on
farming. These concepts acknowledge that agriculture does
not stand apart from the environment of the industrialized
economy.

FARM ORGANIZATIONS IN AN INDUSTRIALIZED ECONOMY

As American agriculture entered the twentieth century the
contradiction between individualism and interdependence was
apparently obscured. An ambivalence was perhaps accommodated
by verbalizing independence as a myth while collectively
eliciting legislative policies that were necessary and advantageous
to commercial agriculture. The popular view of agriculture
as a high calling undergirded these efforts. Moreover, that
agriculture was the foundation of the economy supported
arguments for favorable farm policies.

The Grange

Farmers perfected an array of formal organizations to confront
problems of the twentieth century. The lineage of these
organizations can be traced to the post-Civil War protest groups
which had sought relief from economic hardship by securing
government action. The Grange, organized in 1867 as a social
and fraternal society, provided a structure for the protest
movement when hard times struck western farmers in the
1870's. The Grange, the first large organization initiated, gave
to history the general term "Granger movement" as a reference
to the organizational reaction to economic distress. During the
panic year, 1873, membership and activities rose feverishly, to
return to relative quiescence when the pain of economic distress
subsided. Notwithstanding its sporadic behavior, the Grange left
a legacy of state regulatory acts providing for rate-fixing of
intrastate transportation and storage facilities. It also "left behind
a liberal education in pressure-group procedures for the farm

population on which succeeding agricultural crusades could build."[14]

Though crusading became less stylish as farm organizations matured in later years, the depression of the 1930's coupled with unprecedented drought conditions brought a reenactment of the drama of rural revolt. The Farm Holiday Association exemplifies this sort of action.[15] The direct action techniques of the National Farmers Organization of the 1950's are in the same tradition. The NFO appealed to farm sectors and localities in which individual operators had suffered long-endured losses.

The Farmers Union

The early tradition of the Grange was continued by the Farmers Educational and Cooperative Union of America, better known as the Farmers Union, which appeared in 1902. Basically organized for protest, the Union has adjusted to the realities of American politics, one of the requirements of which is some practice in the art of compromise. With its principal strength located in the Great Plains, this organization keeps protest alive by endorsing slightly left-wing proposals, casting its lot frequently with organized labor, and tilting at the business-educational-agricultural establishment that has become dominant in agricultural life. During times of a Democratic administration in Washington, access of Farmers Union officials to administrative policy-makers increases significantly only to be eclipsed if the Republicans win the presidency. The Farmers Union reconciles agriculture to urbanization by alliances with organized labor. At the same time, it strives to preserve the Jeffersonian ideal of a yeoman class tending toward small-scale equalitarianism.

While the Farmers Union includes well-to-do and conservative farmers in its membership, it conveys the Granger style of protest, through vigorous political activity, with a continuing

---

[14]V. O. Key, Jr., *Politics, Parties and Pressure Groups* (New York: T. Y. Crowell Co., 1952), p. 31.
[15]Carl C. Taylor, *The American Farmers' Movement*, pp. 5–7,

tendency toward attachment to the structure of major
or minor political parties. Thus the Union joined the
Non-Partisan League in North Dakota, a regional short-lived
political party with unorthodox views. Following 1933
the Farmers Union has been related consistently to the
Democratic party, northern branch, but this has not kept locals
from being occasionally dominated by conservative agrarians.
In fact, a fraction of the organization affiliated with the
national presidential campaign of the right-wing Constitutional
Union party for the 1936 election.

American Farm Bureau Federation

The organization that ultimately became the American Farm
Bureau Federation was initiated at a propitious time. As late
as World War I many farmers were still seeking the viable
organization with which to engage nonfarm adversaries. The
Country Life movement sanctioned organization of farmers.
At first glance this is anomalous because agriculture seemed
to be plentifully supplied with organizations. However,
McConnell noted the business inspiration for Farm Bureaus
was a response to the militancy that had been characteristic of
the farmers' movement since the Civil War.[16] Businessmen
had become apprehensive concerning the methods and ends
of farm organizations. Business support apparently
supplied an ingredient that had been lacking in earlier
organizations. In addition, farmers were not novices at forming
organizations. They knew an organization was needed but
it required a different composition from that of its
predecessors. The Farm Bureau was a natural.
Another ingredient, the extension education system of the
land-grant college, completed the formula for the initiation
of this organization. Interestingly enough, as problems have
persisted or proliferated through the years, the techniques
of the Farm Bureau have been successively and successfully

---

[16]Grant McConnell, *The Decline of Agrarian Democracy*
(Berkeley: University of California Press, 1953), p. 164.

refined; confidence has remained unshaken. The Farm
Bureau has become a political power nationally and
in the bulk of the states.

The exercising of political power by an organization whose
objectives are economic is a normal tendency, if judged
by the actions of corporations. Originally, local Farm Bureaus
underwrote the expenses of agricultural technicians sent
from land-grant colleges to educate farmers in better
farming practices. The Smith-Lever Act (1914) authorized
resident county agents to be financed by federal, state,
local, even private funds. Local and state Farm Bureaus
allied with the land-grant college helped provide this aid,
often on a membership-subscription basis. Each partner
ultimately benefited greatly from the alliance. In 1919 the
state organizations combined to form the American Farm
Bureau Federation.

The agricultural county agents cultivated the support of the
organization, and in their 1918 national meeting adopted
resolutions that urged further development of farm bureaus
and their political activity.[17] The growth of the Agricultural
Extension Service and the federated Farm Bureaus
proceeded reciprocally. There were plenty of problems and
resources with which to attack the problems. Ever-expanding
activities propelled these allies to prominence
in agriculture.

The county served as the unit for organizing at the local
level. The county extension agent typically served as secretary
of the local board. Especially was his presence prominent
in the formative stages. These agents' activity in joint efforts
diminished as the lines of demarcation between government
agency and private association were rendered more distinct.[18]

---

[17]Harmon Ziegler, *Interest Groups in American Society*
(Englewood Cliffs: Prentice-Hall, 1964), p. 175.
[18]Federal legislation enacted in 1954 specified the separation of
extension offices from private associations as sponsors or supporters.
The legislation was passed under pressure from organizations
which took a dim view of Extension Service-Farm Bureau
relationships; it of course did not terminate informal relations
based on mutual sympathies and reciprocity.

The political action function of a farm organization may be
better understood if viewed as furthering economic ends
by political means. An economic end sought is the
improvement of farmers' living conditions. Improvement may
be measured against past conditions in agriculture or against
contemporaneous nonfarm sectors of the economy.
Admittedly, the subsectors of agriculture that have political
strength or capacity and can make most efficient use of the
given organization are likely to become dominant and,
therefore, to be the principal beneficiaries of organization
policies. It has been the Farm Bureau's destiny to profit most
from organizing farmers in response to the industrialized
environment.

Farm Cooperatives

Cooperation had been proposed for a century as a solution to
the farmers' problems. Elaborate schemes of cooperation were
instigated by the Grange and other farm organizations.
During the first two decades of the twentieth century
cooperatives became more numerous and by the third decade
cooperatives were firmly included in the American farmer's
financial armament. Some measure of the rapidity of
growth is indicated by changes between 1915 and 1925. In
that period the number of farr..er cooperatives almost doubled,
total memberships quadrupled to 2,700,000, and dollar volume
more than trebled to 2.4 billion.[19] During the third decade
farmer cooperatives were preferred by some farm groups as
an alternative to the seeking of legislation favorable to
agriculture. In this context, farm cooperatives were an
empirical collective response to agricultural problems which
did not require that farmers solicit support from government.
Farmer-controlled state legislatures, beginning with Wisconsin
in 1911, enacted statutes favoring cooperative marketing of

---

[19]Anne L. Gessner, *Statistics of Farmer Cooperatives,* 1960–61,
General Report 112 (Washington: F.C.S., U.S. Department
of Agriculture, 1963), pp. 14, 74.

farm products and encouraged the formation of rural
consumer cooperatives. In 1922, Congress bestowed
special privileges upon farmers' cooperatives in freeing
them from liabilities under the antitrust laws. Ironically,
antitrust laws had been passed under the pressure
of agrarian protest. The cooperative seemed to be a means of
overcoming the farmer's disadvantage in the market economy.
Farmers were willing to qualify their traditional laissez-faire
philosophy further and acclaimed the establishment in 1926
of a Division of Cooperatives in the U.S. Department of
Agriculture under the Cooperative Marketing Act.
In 1929, Congress established a supervised revolving
fund of $500,000,000—the Farm Board—to advance funds to
agricultural cooperative marketing associations. Federal farm
enactments of the 1920's were responses to the generally depressed
condition of commercial agriculture.

These enactments do not include all of the political
acquisitions achieved for cooperatives. For example, a farm
cooperative statistical series commenced in 1913. Also, the host
agency for the statistical series—the United States Department
of Agriculture—further implicated the executive branch
of the federal government in buttressing rural living. It has
been observed that farm cooperatives were an alternative to
seeking amelioration through legislative action. It was
evident that the executive branch, in this example, and in the
instance of partial federal financing of county agent work,
had become sensitized to act directly on farmers' problems.
In essence, these examples of intervention were consistent with
recommendations of the Country Life Commission.

By 1950 the nearly ten thousand farmer cooperatives
constituted a significant force in rural life. Marketing coops
outnumbered the purchasing coops about two to one and
accounted for three out of four dollars farmers obtained by
participation. The cooperative device has been of great
significance in developing rural electrical facilities under loans
from the Rural Electrification Administration.

Undoubtedly, the protective legislation and executive action extended to farm cooperatives reflects ideological preference for agrarian life. The vigorous attacks upon their favored status likewise reflects the conflicting ideology of business enterprise. Numerous court cases have dealt with the position of farmer cooperatives but have not disposed of the issues with clarity. It appears that an agricultural marketing association might legitimately gain and hold control of 100 percent of a given commodity market, if its conduct was free from restraint of trade or predatory practices. Such an action by a private enterprise association would be in violation of antitrust law.

A successful business is measured by its growth. Cooperatives have become big businesses. Noting the agrarian's traditional distrust of centralization, cooperative leaders have aggressively developed the philosophy that bigness combined with cooperatives is good, not bad.

A case in point is the Consumers Cooperative Association of Kansas City, Missouri. The thirty-sixth annual meeting—1964—was attended by 7,739 persons. Voting delegates represented over seven hundred local associations. CCA's annual volume was one-quarter of a billion dollars with net savings of nearly 17 million. The President reported:

We are involved in the biggest expansion program CCA has ever undertaken at one time. . . . Farming must adapt itself to its industrial environment. . . . It must become a part of industry to the extent necessary to provide farmers an equitable return on their labor and capital. And it is only through cooperatives that farmers can merge their operations with those of industry without being swallowed up in the process.[20]

---

[20]*Cooperative Consumer* (Kansas City, Missouri), December 31, 1964. CCA savings were disposed of as follows:
$1,706.852 was paid in cash as dividends on preferred stock.
$1,912,600 was set aside to pay state and federal income taxes.
$984.855 was assigned to consolidated earned surplus.
$12,177,366 was allocated for patronage refunds due CCA patrons.
The refunds were treated as follows:
$6,026.183 was reinvested for patrons in CCA common stock.
$125,000 was paid for member association subscriptions to *The Cooperative Consumer*.
$6,026,183 was paid to patrons in cash.

CCA resolutions encouraged expansion of the cooperative's investment in processing industries in order to provide a complete, local one-stop service center for all farm supplies. Such cooperatives tend to be interested in every phase of rural life and furnish a focus of integration that is powerful for those who participate successfully.

Commodity groups are important organizations in a modern agriculture. These organizations manifest the vigor of the drive toward specialization in farming. On the one hand, the agricultural way of life has come to include public programs that collect and publicize analyses of the production and marketing of commercial farmers. The scale of public attention manifests the societal relevance of agriculture. On the other hand, the best liaison between public policy-maker and private decision-maker has been in many instances the special purpose commodity organizations. These organizations articulate with the highly specified needs of their members.

The commodity groups serve to indicate the theory and ideology on which modern American agriculture operates. A system that rewards large-scale production of specialized products encourages the formation of comparable associative organizations. The almost innumerable commodity organizations pursue specific goals, whereas the more general farm organizations engage in adjusting the competing demands of their constituent parts. Each kind of organization tends to represent the interest of commercial farmers in the industrialized environment.

THE ORGANIZED AND DIFFERENTIATED RURAL COMMUNITY

This chapter has depicted agriculture as it became implicated in an industrialized urbanized environment: one feature was that farm pressure groups had successfully obtained public support for commercial farmers. We shall now consider the thrust of modern agriculture within the confines of the generalized rural community. What effects did the commercialization and specialization of production, the introduction of public programs, and the legislative gains have on local communities?

World War I has been designated as the point of origin for the modern version of American agriculture. Genung noted that the demands of the war affected agricultural development and public policy as well.[21] Mechanization of production increased yields at the time that foreign markets contracted following the close of the war. The optimism of agriculturists, which had been verified by rising prices since the mid-1890's, was replaced by pessimism engendered by the postwar farm depression. While many changes could have resulted from other pressures, more dynamism was compressed into fewer years in this era than American farmers had ever before experienced. Government had importuned or solicited farmers into acting in the wartime period. Apparently this was a prime part of the county agent's job. At any rate, a reversal of roles may be noted: previously, farmers had solicited government.

The agricultural depression that followed the armistice resulted in vehement organized protest from American farmers. Organizations served American farmers well in this crisis. Moreover, in a new form of structure, several farm organizations united in a council to speak in a unified voice for agriculture. Coordinated efforts proved to be successful in the attainment of certain objectives. A slogan of the 1920's— "equality for agriculture"—persisted as a viable symbol for a generation of farmers.

Farmers sought "equality" because business and industry had not suffered as agriculture had on the return of peace. Equality would ultimately require government subsidization of agriculture in the field of credit and in areas related to production and marketing; that subsidization was involved may have stalled legislation or it may have

---

[21]A. B. Genung, "Agriculture in the World War Period," *Farmers in a Changing World, Yearbook of Agriculture, 1940* (Washington: U.S. Government Printing Office, 1940), p. 295.

caused approved bills to be vetoed by the executive. This
decade was the period when ideas for amelioration of
agriculture's problems were proposed. The last year of the
decade, a crop storage scheme—the Farm Board—was initiated.

Government Intervention in the 1930's

The 1930's were characterized by intervention on a massive
scale. Farm production controls, soil conservation, rural
electrification, resettlement homesteads, special assistance to
low-income farmers, a tenant purchase program exemplify the
range of attention. The prolonged agricultural depression,
drought, the acknowledged breaks in the "agricultural
ladder," the low levels of living among farmers as compared with
city dwellers, and other problems, contributed to government's
attentiveness to agriculture.

The new legislation was implemented through action agencies.
Not all of these were originally in the United States Department
of Agriculture; some were independent or in other executive
branches. However, by the close of the 1930's, almost all
agencies having to do with agriculture had been collected under
the mantle of the USDA. Some agencies maintained local
offices and staffs that allowed access to rural communities
and neighborhoods. Their personnel engaged in activities
largely concerning farm production.

The Resettlement Administration and the Farm Security
Administration supported agrarianism in a new fashion: they
constituted a rural analogue of the welfare-oriented urban
relief programs.[22] These agencies' clientele were low-income
persons in rural areas. Commercial operators who choose not
to accept relief or did not require relief were galled by this
and other relief programs.[23] They were especially critical of
relief programs if they raised laborers' wages.

---

[22]Horace Miner, *Culture and Agriculture* (Ann Arbor:
University of Michigan Press, 1949), Chapter 5.
[23]*Ibid.*, pp. 82-48; Walter Goldschmidt, *As You Sow* (New York:
Harcourt, Brace and Co., 1947), p. 184.

The action agencies most popular with commercial farmers were those concerned with improving productivity or rewarding potential productivity. Action agencies which had social objectives—relief programs, programs for laborers or low-income farmers—apparently departed too much from production emphasis. The action agency, however, manifests the new operational character of government agencies in rural communities; personnel obtained rationales for actions to be taken which had not necessarily been solicited by farmers.

A local committee of farmers ordinarily advised employees of the government agencies. By and large, these advisory committees represented the commercial, owner-operating farmers in the county. Goldschmidt observed that even though "labor" was an important subject to the farmers in California's Central Valley, no farm laborers were included in committees that planned farm programs.[24] Miner observed that ordinary farm tenants were not a part of the Farm Security Administration advisory committee that chose candidates for the county's tenant purchase plan.[25] The advisory committee, by including only farmers of a single status, probably enhanced an agency's entry into the local area and assisted in obtaining consensus between local residents and agency representatives. In essence, partly private and partly public sponsorship was obtained by use of this device.

Restructuring of access was not unopposed. Apparently the Farm Bureau and the land-grant colleges attempted to encapsulate the action agencies while the USDA attempted to enlarge its beachhead. The Mount Weather Agreement of 1938 effected a compromise whereby Land Use Planning would enter rural counties through the Cooperative Extension Services. The USDA agency for social science research— the Bureau of Agricultural Economics—had the responsibility

---

[24]*Ibid*, p. 174.
[25]Miner, *Culture and Agriculture*, p. 91n.

to furnish the empirically based rationales for land use
planning.

This program departed from previous farm programs in that
planning was to involve the rural community and was
not to deal exclusively with farm production. Thus, it seems
reasonable to have used a social science agency to oversee
the action. However, it was not prudent to utilize the agency
which was also involved in social science research. Land Use
Planning, allegedly a democratic partnership between farm
people and the federal government, was a casualty of World
War II. During the war the Farm Bureau was the most effective
organization dealing with the United States Congress. It was
able to emasculate this work and other programs that varied from
the Farm Bureau's objectives.[26]

During the war a policy dialogue occurred between two
protagonists: the Farm Bureau and social-science spokesmen of
the USDA. Social scientists emphasized human environmental
variables as they discussed farmers and farming, while Farm
Bureau spokesmen emphasized individual variables of
innateness and inherent nature. On the one hand, the
low-income farmer could be improved by specialized attention
and training; and on the other, he was poor because he deserved
to be so and special attention would not be worth the
expenditure.[27] The dialogue manifested two approaches to the
rural community and two views of human nature. It also showed
that the rural community was not homogeneous.

The dialogue clarified and illuminated the views of rural
America that were held by the protagonists. Public
policy for agriculture has been only slightly modified from
that established by 1938.[28] Perhaps restrictions on changes
in farm policy were successful beyond the World War II years.

---

[26]Charles M. Hardin, "The Bureau of Agricultural Economics
Under Fire, *Journal of Farm Economics,* 28, No. 3 (1946),
635–668; Neal C. Gross, "A Post Mortem on County Planning,"
Journal of Farm Economics, 25, No. 3 (1943), 644–61.
[27]Hardin, "The B.A.E. Under Fire."
[28]Wayne D. Rasmussen, "The Impact of Technological Change
on Agriculture, 1862–1962," *Journal of Economic History,*
22, No. 4 (1963), 578–91.

Rasmussen also noted that agricultural technology has so elaborated in the period that different policies are required. The next policy innovations, if the Rural Development, Rural Areas Development, and Rural Poverty Programs are indicative, will probably apply some recommendations of Land Use Planning.

Another Element in the Supportive Institution:
The Land-grant Colleges

Numerous external agencies have become implicated in the rural community.[29] The extension service is the agency of the land-grant institution that enters rural communities.

The extension worker, in contrast to the researcher or the classroom teacher cannot ignore the ideological dispositions of the people with whom he works. The extension worker may favor or oppose agrarianism; he cannot ignore it.

The extension service sought to improve "backward" farmers.[30] Today, "underdeveloped" would be used. The extension service was a social invention that provided educational materials and an instructor to aid in their interpretation and application.

With reference to procedural methods used, Lord observed that money-making programs—an emphasis on solving problems of production—were temporarily suitable in a time when farmers were poor and driven.[31] Lord believed that the original orientation, however, did not have the substance to prevail as a long-run viable rationale for extension work.

The extension system has continued to emphasize production problems. (In recent years it has become fashionable to talk about broadening this program. However, many would contend

---

[29]The limited view we follow excludes many other organizations that are involved in the rural community: religious denominations, numerous federal and state agencies, and business, industrial, and labor organizations also pay attention to agriculture.

[30]Goldschmidt, *As You Sow,* p. 239.

[31]Russell Lord. *The Agrarian Revival* (New York: George Grady Press, 1939), pp. 182–83.

that broadening has not in fact occurred. Extension has affiliated with commercial farmers rather than with low-income farmers and with the more highly capitalized farmers in the commercial category. Vidich and Bensman write:

The county agent, with his interests in innovation, efficiency, modernization and rational business-like farming, is psychologically oriented to the rational prosperous farmers. The very life style and farming methods of the traditional farmer leave the program of the county agent without any appeal.[32]

Several years earlier West noted that those who acted as experts in introducing new agricultural practices to Plainvillers brought a new way of life to the residents. He referred to the farmers who accepted the agricultural innovations as "farming rationalists."[33] If traditional farming is compatible with farming as a way of life, then rationality is compatible with farming as a business. In other words, the rational farmer would regard his land and livestock as investments from which financial returns could be realized rather than in sentimental or mystical or status-conferring terms.

The farm programs, in attempting to make rural life equal to urban life, encouraged government subsidy and assistance. Farmers were subsidized to practice scientific or nontraditional agriculture. West observes that three revolutionary occurrences —the improved steel plow, the automobile, and scientific agriculture—significantly changed Plainville.[34] Scientific agriculture differed in its introduction to the residents from the other two in such a drastic way as to render it an innovation in another dimension; the federal government introduced it and farmers were financially assisted to make some required adjustments.

Extension and other government programs had become so associated with the introduction of innovations that, Gallaher

---

[32]Arthur J. Vidich and Joseph Bensman, *Small Town in Mass Society* (Princeton: Princeton University Press, 1958), p. 214.
[33]James West, *Plainville, U.S.A.* (New York: Columbia University Press, 1945), p. 224.
[34]*Ibid.*, p. 218.

noted in his restudy of Plainville, the agents of these programs were criticized when they failed to advocate new ideas.[35] We may now observe that apparently a second fundamental change had occurred in the relationship between farmers and the intervening public agencies. The first, it will be recalled, involved the reversal of the ameliorative sequence: government personnel advocating action for rural or farm people in place of self-advocacy on the part of the aggrieved. Gallaher's conclusion that agency personnel were expected to advocate new ideas would indicate that for many farmers traditional agriculture was insufficient as a viable answer to the job of farming. Technicians who assisted farmers to farm became a resource to be incorporated in the farm enterprise.

The relationship between the extension service and the Farm Bureau has been widely documented. McConnell stated that the Farm Bureau's growth was mightily affected by the parallel development of the county agent system, that the Bureau resisted USDA agencies seeking to organize local affiliates because it feared the growth of a competitive farm organization from these units, and that the Farm Bureau gained more from the relationship than did extension.[36]

Knowledge of human affairs suggests that mutually affiliated organizations are more likely to be peers than to be unequals in joint endeavors. It is difficult to visualize an unequal pattern secularly persisting. A persisting pattern of unequals, a dominant-colonial arrangement, requires differences between the superordinate and the subordinate—differences, for example, in technological equipment, literacy, skilled manpower, and human organization. Moreover, this unequal situation involves discrimination and an unequal distribution of rewards. We suggest it is reasonable to conclude that each party in the Farm Bureau-extension service combination obtained, indeed obtains, sufficient rewards to encourage it to continue in joint

[35] Art Gallaher, *Plainville Revisited* (New York: Columbia University Press, 1961), p. 244.
[36] McConnell, *The Decline of Agrarian Democracy*, pp. 176–77.

ventures. It is unlikely that discrimination characterizes the relationship.

The view that the Farm Bureau is "guiltier" than is the extension service for its involvement in the relationship is analogous to the view that the man is guiltier than is the woman when a common-law marriage produces a bastard child. An allegation of more or less guilt requires the application of a double standard. The long-time affiliation considered here presents an additional inexplicable departure from conventional American behavior. In American society, the idea that Caesar's wife must be above suspicion and reproach is more frequently applied against the public employee when he is apprehended in a questionable arrangement with a private citizen than it is applied against the private individual. The public servant is expected to be circumspect while a certain latitude is accorded the private man. Yet, the extension service's remaining innocent contradicts this American convention.

Accounting for these discrepancies lies beyond our province for the present. However, conjectural hypotheses are presented. Perhaps observers depict the Farm Bureau as sinner and extension a nonsinner because in the one instance evidence is tangible and in the other it is not. The Farm Bureau's record of lobbying is a matter of public information while extension's actions vis-à-vis political actions have been more appropriately those of the silent partner. Or perhaps the observers have been overly generous toward extension because they have closer kinship with the educational organization than they have with the voluntary association. We see flaws in others that we do not observe in ourselves or in our kin. Or perhaps both the Farm Bureau and extension have served to secure legislative gains or support for the land-grant system as a whole in each of several states and nationally as well. In this instance access to rural areas and their legislators is obtained by the joint arrangement. Meanwhile nonextension administrators have reaped the benefits of legislative entree without being directly involved in the seemingly nonacademic

behavior which special pleaders use. In this latter instance each
of the partners has in turn been used by a third party.

Our remarks on the land-grant institution will be concluded
by reference to the observations of two economists:

Boulding characterized the land-grant system as having been
antithetical to agricultural fundamentalism.[37] He noted that
the success of the agricultural arm of the system associated with
increasing the efficiency of farming. Or, stating this another
way: As the agricultural college succeeded in achieving its
objectives, a steadily diminishing farm population was a
consequence. Some decried this development. Perhaps they
reasoned from the ironic analogy that is exemplified in the case
of the able workman who by following highly efficient methods
worked himself out of a job. However, it seems more valid
to applaud the part played by this system in achieving
efficient production.

Wilson has demonstrated confidence in the land-grant
system, citing its legacy of the acceptance of innovation
as a foundation for continuing acceptance of other innovations.[38]
He noted that the system characteristically adapted to change
in its first fifty years. However, its second fifty years were
characterized by attachment to the status quo. If this system
returns to its earlier tendency of adapting and contributing to
change by identification with a venturing, inquiring spirit,
then Wilson's confidence will be well placed.

HARVESTS OF MODERNIZATION AND ORGANIZATION

The modernization of agriculture and the organization of the
rural community, leading forces for fifty years, have ramified
beyond farming and the agricultural locale. While the

---

[37]Kenneth Boulding, "Agricultural Organization and Policies:
A Personal Evaluation," *Farm Goals in Conflict,* (Ames:
Iowa State University Press, 1963).
[38]C. Peairs Wilson, "The Emerging Role of the Land Grant System
in Domestic Growth and Adjustment," address delivered to the
Southwestern Social Science Association (n.d.).

urban-industrial sectors heavily influence farming, tremors
within the lesser part—agriculture—eddy into the larger
society. The anecdote to be described now, concerning the
controversial reaction to a television presentation on
contemporary rural America, illustrates urban-rural
interdependence. The second section describes a
social-political development in the rural community.

The Land: a Portrayal of Rural America

In 1962, the National Broadcasting Company executed
a television documentary entitled *The Land* that probed
rural life. The program ironically portrayed abundant
farm yields as concomitants of catastrophe. The modernized
farm, ever expanding its borders and its uses of machinery
under the application of technology, was pictured as a
champion of efficient production. However, the necessary
merging of a multitude of homesteads to form the modern
unit was a pessimistic undertone to the theme of optimism.
The delineation of irony was clear: greater surpluses
flowed from fewer hands.

One catastrophe depicted was the poignant portrayal of
small farmers selling out and moving to the city. The
commentator noted that the city, with its unemployment rolls,
might not be a reasonable alternative. Another portrayal
showed undisplaced small farmers struggling to earn a living
in surroundings rendered ever more alien by feats of
technology. A manifest consequence emanating from these
actions was the diminution of customers for farm trade centers.
Exhibitions of several declining farm trade centers dramatized
census statistics; hence the belief was substantiated that
the cases depicted were neither sensational nor exceptional.
The program's commentator, Chet Huntley, was pictured in
the Montana village in which he had been born. Each scene
underscored social costs farm communities have paid and are
paying because they offer too few comparative opportunities.

The Land credited the knowledge-developing and
information-disseminating functions of the land-grant university

as agents of productivity gains. Surely these institutions have played a substantial role in the gains. Campus scenes featured research activities underway that would be translated into improved methods of processing and producing food and fibre. Other campus and rural scenes emphasized that few college students with farm backgrounds would return home upon graduation. Apparently they would follow Mr. Huntley's lead to urban residence.

Prerelease publicity on *The Land* implicated a leading land-grant university—Kansas State—in the forthcoming program. Kansas commentators—news media persons, highly placed leaders—directed negative views toward Kansas State because conclusions of its area development research group provided the initial impetus for the program. A fear was expressed that *The Land* would derogate and ridicule Kansas. The rash of prejudgments apparently inhibited the University's administration from capitalizing on a remarkable public relations event.

Those who waited to express their conclusions until the program had been presented and who expressed their sentiments in letter form were overwhelmingly favorable.[39] The program clarified agricultural problems; much that had occurred on "the land" had previously been obscured; some observed that the Jeffersonian thesis had not been realized despite public attention to farmers.

This episode illustrated two points. The selection of the topic and the comments on the program confirmed the

---

[39]The present authors were members of the research group. When it became apparent that the program was to be a "cause" we obtained the mail, except for those letters that had been directed to the sponsor, that had been sent in response to *The Land*. The mail the sponsor received, which was analyzed by the sponsor, was 92 percent favorable. The mail available to us was analyzed. Of the nearly 400 letters—an unusually large response according to several observers—89 percent was favorable. Moreover, a substantial fraction of the 11 percent that had not expressed a favorable reaction were neutral expressions. For example, some writers requested information as to availability of a print of the film. The 22 letters that bore a Kansas return address were *all* favorable.

relevance of agrarianism. Further, Huntley's rural origin exemplified a background often found in urban life. This sensitive commentator transmitted the rural dream and nightmare to the nation. The second point illustrated the nature of the dilemma that confronts many nonfarm organizations that have investments in agriculture. These organizations—and in this instance a single university represents numerous agencies or organizations—readily accept authorship for productivity gains while denying authorship for some consequences of the gains. The following section will consider reasons for this denial.

The Excluded Segment in the Organized Community

Social differentiation of the rural community has already been noted. Some additional details are required to complete the canvas. It has been apparent for at least a generation that approximately one-half of the farmers contributed all of the production marketed by American farms.[40] Taylor and Jones noted recently that less than three percent of all farms accounted for more than one-fourth of the marketed products.[41] Perhaps more than one-half of the farm population is redundant in the present system. This fraction of farmers could disappear with no noticeable effect on the flow of products to market.

Hamilton observed that rural residence is desirable for four reasons, of which only one concerns the farm as a production enterprise.[42] Moreover, he noted that as urban-industrial expansion continues, increasing predominance will be given to preferences other than the opportunity afforded by commercial farm production. Rural residents will seek subsistence, security, or privacy which

---

[40]Raymond C. Smith, "New Conditions Demand New Opportunities," *Farmers in a Changing World, Yearbook of Agriculture, 1940* (Washington: U.S. Government Printing Office, 1940), p. 816.
[41]Lee Taylor and Arthur R. Jones, Jr., *Rural Life and Urbanized Society* (New York: Oxford University Press, 1964), p. 294.
[42]C. Horace Hamilton, "The Sociology of a Changing Agriculture," *Social Forces*, 37, No. 1 (1958), 1–7.

can be obtained in the open country. The farm community has become a rural community, in which many residents no longer have a commercial interest in agriculture.

Public agencies whose employees work in agriculture have been influenced by the differentiated community. McConnell noted that professional workers preferred to work with commercial farmers and by virtue of this selective attention the gap between successful and unsuccessful farmers widened.[43] The entry of public agencies into the farm community was influenced by the community's composition, and differentiation grew apace with the operations of the agencies.

The pronounced penchants of private and public organizations related to agriculture for marketing cooperatives and for viewing the farm problem in a production-price context met the needs of commercial farmers. Within the group of public agencies, McConnell also observed, the Farm Security Administration, which actually upheld the agrarian tradition—the furthering of farm ownership opportunities for low-income farmers— received miniscule support for its activities.[44] As a matter of fact, public programs that have had the entire rural community as their target—Land Use Planning, Rural Development—have not been supported by the powerful spokesmen who have articulated agrarianism. Perhaps support has been withheld because the interests of commercial agriculture are not preeminent in these programs, or perhaps nonsupport is grounded in the belief that another program would dissipate the public's attention to agriculture.

One segment within the differentiated community—the commercial farmers—has incorporated the professional workers' expertise into their enterprises. Inferring from the literature, one could observe that graduates of land-grant schools are generally insensitive to the problems of marginal farmers. Inasmuch as professional workers in agriculture are recruited

---

[43]McConnell, *The Decline of Agrarian Democracy*, p. 166.
[44]*Ibid.*, p. 88.

from this educational system it is fair to assume that public
agency employees have difficulty establishing rapport with poor
farmers. The union between expert worker and commercial
farmer is not a sinister bargain, it is simply an equal-status
contact easy to effect. They share common ideas and agree on
numerous issues. A co-opted relationship ensues: it is
immaterial which partner initiated the relationship.[45]

Perhaps two field work experiences in the tobacco-producing
area of southern Maryland will illustrate details of the culture
of low-income farmers. One farmer owned more than 160 acres
of land free and clear. Yet he cultivated less than ten
acres, which were devoted to tobacco and corn. He was not
motivated to cultivate, graze, or tree-farm his owned wasteland
because the cropland yielded sufficient income for his needs. His
behavior would be reprehensible or unintelligible to the average
technical agricultural worker. However, he had free time
to hunt and fish and exercise whims that lay outside the scope
of earning a living.

Another farmer owned a substantial tract of standing timber.
A timber buyer (our information came from the buyer and was
later verified as accurate) determined that timber to be cut from
the tract would be worth $9,000. However, the buyer, in
a bargaining context, decided to make an initial offer of
$2,000 to the farmer. The buyer was aghast when the farmer
accepted. In this instance, the farmer had no comprehension
of the market. Furthermore, the farm owner was apparently
unaware that his state's forestry agency would provide
technical advice concerning the cutting of timber on his
land and would give him some idea as to the value of
his timber. These were free services.

The modernization of agriculture and the organization of
the rural community have been attended by some strain
and tension. We will now turn to the empirical task of
describing and analyzing agrarianism in specified instances.

---

[45]Philip Selznick, *TVA and the Grass Roots* (Berkeley: University
of California Press, 1949), pp. 259–61, for the nature of co-optation.

4

THE PUBLIC
SECTOR
OF
RURAL LIFE

The first view of public policy toward agriculture reveals a
national government organized and directed to promote the
well-being of this sector of the economy. This view is partially
correct. One of the results of the peculiarly favored position
of men of the land in the American heritage has been to make
them the beneficiary of an array of national policies. The
generosity of federal policies toward already prospering farmers
has been a popular topic. One commentator, for example, wrote:

Everybody knows that it is the taxpayer who keeps the farmers
(or rather, a favored group of them) living in clover and
Cadillacs. . . . The Treasury spent nearly $3 billion during
the last fiscal year to support farm prices—but that was just the
beginning. The scheme is rigged to nick the taxpayer twice; once
when he pays to take surplus crops off the market, thus propping
up prices; and again when he has to pay these artificial
prices at the grocery store.[1]

---

[1]John Fischer, "The Country Slickers Take Us Again," *Harper's,*
211 (December 1955), 21.

The development of rural public institutions and values cannot be understood by analysis of national policy alone, however. As evidence now available clearly indicates, the generosity of national policy in agriculture has been inversely related to need.[2] Correspondingly, many farm people of the United States have displayed ingenuity in taking advantage,of local institutions and conventions and adjusting living habits to the continuing situation. This adjustment has included development and strengthening of the pattern of political behavior generally recognized as rural conservatism. The tensions between conservatism and progressivism and the reconciliation of these contradictory styles of political behavior among agriculturists constitute an important area for observation and analysis.

Vidich and Bensman note the significant differences between types of farmers and classify them into "rational" and "traditional" types.[3] The rational farmers are those who have developed the scientific, technological, and commercial aspects of farming. "Rationality rather than sentiment or tradition governs the work and mentality of rational farmers." On the other hand, traditional farmers are those for whom "farming is a way of life to be practiced in all its ceremonial and ritual complexity." The traditional farmers resist technological innovations and increases of scale which tie the farm operator to "outside" economic forces—that is, make him a dependent and specialized part of the vast complex of modern economic life.

While these are observable types in agricultural society, and the traditional farmer is in a peculiar sense the custodian of historic American agrarianism, an additional dimension needs to be added. It was noted earlier that agrarianism has particular connotations applicable on the one hand to the public or civic

---

[2] Cf. Edward C. Higbee, *Farms and Farmers in an Urban Age* (New York: Twentieth Century Fund, 1963); Walter R. Goldschmidt, *As You Sow*, 1st ed. (New York: Harcourt, Brace and Co., 1947), pp. 245-62.

[3] Arthur J. Vidich and Joseph Bensman, *Small Town in Mass Society: Class, Power, and Religion in a Rural Community* (Princeton: Princeton University Press, 1958), pp. 55–69.

life, on the other to the private or economic. By plotting these on intersecting continua, additional categories are identifiable that aid in understanding the way in which the civic life has made an important and distinctive contribution to the agrarian tradition.

The horizontal axis in Figure I marks the separation of farmers into the two types, traditional and rational, delineated above. As the figure suggests, the categories are not discrete and extreme, but rather graduated with varying intermixtures of traditionalism and rationalism, from one extreme to the other. A pure example of either type is hard to find.

Let the vertical axis represent a continuum upward from little local governments with much autonomy to big impersonal units characterized by specialists and bureaucracy. In his book, *Grass Roots,* Martin has sketched the distinction between little or

FIGURE I.   CLEAVAGES IN AGRARIANISM: TRANSITION VARIABLES
            IN PUBLIC AND PRIVATE SECTORS

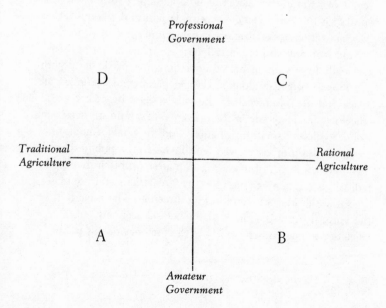

"amateur" government and big, professional government.[4] The former are comparable on the public front to traditional farms on the private. However, there is little congruence between the two in reality. The development of mechanized and large-scale commercial agriculture has been almost independent of the local development of specialized and professional government, and the latter has lagged in time behind the former.

Each of the sectors *A, B, C,* and *D* in Figure I presents a segment of the farm population, both in environmental and in aspirational or preferential terms. Sectors *A* and *C* present compatibility of private and civic situations and preferences. That is, in *A* are found those traditional farmers whose public lives are also traditionalist in the sense that they are related with and integrated with small rural units of local government. Not only do substantial numbers of farmers live this type of situation but also there are many values and preferences associated with self-sufficiency and locally autonomous government. Declining communities, in an extreme form exemplified by Appalachia, are representative of sector *A*. In sector *C* is found the diametrically opposing condition, one that speaks for the American concept of agricultural modernization. Mechanization, specialization, expansion of scale, both in the private economy and organization of government, prevail. An especially high value is placed upon progress, particularly with an emphasis upon production. Larger production in the private sector finds its counterpart in the public sector in greater efficiency and economy in the operation of administrative units. Consolidation of small jurisdictions and the establishment of special authorities are viewed with favor. In the public sphere, the above standards of modernization are most often met by the federal government, though local consolidations and use of special authorities also tend in that direction. The force that the Farm Bureau sometimes places behind economy and efficiency in government indicates the presence of this public

---

[4]Roscoe C. Martin, *Grass Roots* (University, Ala.: University of Alabama Press, 1957).

value.[5] Areas of rapidly growing populations with large agricultural components are representative of Sector C.

Sectors B and D in Figure I represent mixed, i.e., conflicting positions. One might therefore suppose that these areas would not be populated, that if an agricultural situation was advanced in production technology, or "rationalized" economically, it would not contain the kind of public life we have characterized as traditional or amateur. And it might also be hypothesized that the reverse arrangement would not occur.

But, as has been said, there is not a perfect, or even an approximate, congruence between public and private sectors. In the first place, given the pluralistic nature of American federalism, the governmental arrangements may present both styles in the same area simultaneously. And considering only local government, one of its pervasive characteristics in rural areas is its adherence to traditional forms long after the farms have gone far in productive and marketing technology. Readily available data as well as much of the general literature in farm economics indicate that Sector B is heavily populated. Particularly in the midwest and Great Plains regions of the United States, agricultural technology has far outstripped governmental modernization. The role of traditional government, in a modern setting, therefore, requires careful analysis.

Conditions applicable to Sector B are found in much of American agricultural society, but Sector D embraces a deviant, though by no means unknown, condition. Here are found those who subscribe to and derive support from modernized government while maintaining traditional small farm units. Here one finds, too, corresponding value preferences which reflect faintly nostalgic appreciation of rusticity, but not to the extent of foregoing professionalism in public administration, as,

---

[5]One Farm Bureau official who was discussing legislative reapportionment ingeniously proposed that counties should be consolidated for administrative purposes, but for these purposes only, leaving the original boundaries to provide the units for legislative representation. Supreme Court opinions on equal apportionment have invalidated this proposal.

for example, hospital services, hard-surface roads, highway
safety patrols, and the like. Many of the farm hobbyists qualify
for occupancy of this sector. Likewise, fringe settlements around
suburbia sometimes partake of this condition.

Although it is not at present a dominant part of the agricultural
population, this group, nevertheless, typifies a way of life and
an ideology of interest. To the extent that the good life is held
to include elements of agrarianism but also at the same time
elements of urban-centered technology, this combination seems
to represent maximum goal-values.[6] Its weakness, obviously, is
on the production front where the major farm issues have been
thought to reside.

An economic interpretation of differentiation within agriculture
is descriptively accurate but does not reflect the complexities
of attitudes and behavior that prevail in rural America.[7] As
Vidich and Bensman have pointed out, a dominant equalitarian
attitude has prevailed, notwithstanding the stress of extremely
disparate incomes.[8] The pluralism of American public life
facilitates a differentiation which accommodates the economic
extremes while at the same time the tradition of equality is
perpetuated. A breakdown of this equilibrium, such as may be
found in the Appalachian region, is symptomatic of profound
dislocations in the social system.

Within this setting, the political forces that operate in agrarian
life can be understood, their apparent contradictions reconciled,
and the range of available alternatives for American agrarianism
better described. With the framework thus provided, it is
possible to discuss in meaningful terms the major characteristics
and relationships found in the government and politics of
agrarian America.

---

[6]Most serious analyses of contemporary agriculture ignore this
arrangement. However, see Leon H. Keyserling, *Agriculture
and the Public Interest: Toward a New Farm Program*
(Washington: Conference on Economic Progress, 1965).

[7]Higbee, *Farms and Farmers in an Urban Age*, Chapter 2;
Goldschmidt, *As You Sow*, Chapter IX.

[8]Vidich and Bensman, *Small Town in Mass Society*, pp. 40–42.

Lancaster wrote that rural government as such seemed about to disappear from America.[9] This possibility seems remote when one analyzes in some depth the social forces that have developed within public agricultural policy. In the nearly thirty years that have passed since this observation, the forms of rural government have undergone some, though not striking, changes. If by rural government, we mean little or amateur governments, as Lancaster did not and Martin, writing later, did (see p. 81), then a tendency for their replacement with big or professional government is observable. This is a slow trend, however, and is, in itself, a change in form frequently lacking in strength to displace rural values and symbols.[10] Perhaps the presence of a trend toward change represents effects that state and national levels have on local government.

The primary nature of civic agrarianism in present-day American life can be brought out by an analysis of current issues that are matters of contention on this front. The gravest of these is the legislative reapportionment issue; of much significance also are reorganization of local governments, especially school districts, and the increasing scope of governmental functions and services. Governmental pluralism adds importance to differential popular acceptance of these activities at various levels, local, state, and national.

RURAL PLURALISM

Local government has been subjected to the impact of declining population throughout rural America. This steady drain of human resources has been accompanied by an increasing farm productivity resulting from the application of technology. This, in itself, has created problems. As social and economic life becomes more complex, pressures on government to provide

---

[9]Lane Lancaster, *Government in Rural America* (New York: D. Van Nostrand Company, 1937), pp. 20-23.
[10]R. G. Klietsch *et al., Social Response to Population Change and Migration,* North Central Regional Research Report No. 153 (Ames: Iowa Agricultural Experiment Station, 1964).

new and better services mount. Local government, cast in the
traditional forms, responds very inadequately to these demands.
Part of this inadequacy stems, of course, from the nature of
the local units; more fundamental, however, is the fact that the
traditional style of local government has remained responsive
to certain sets of needs that are of importance to traditional
farmers.

It is noteworthy that the political maps of most counties and
states in the United States have provided a basis for the
development of the civic culture advocated by Jefferson. In
most cases, counties were of a convenient size, even in terms of
pre-automobile travel. Within counties, townships were
frequently given governmental status by relatively simple
legislative procedures. And within or overlapping townships,
special-purpose districts have been generously provided. This
arrangement offers a contrast with local government systems in
other nations, such as those of Spanish or Continental origin.
In the Philippines, for example, the towns embrace rural and
village areas contiguously throughout whole provinces, playing
down the tendency toward multiple self-governing units.[11]

The areas thus laid out for rural local government lost their
utility to the predominant culture of technology and
urbanization; they have continued to serve the subordinate
strata of traditional farmers and village businessmen and
shopkeepers. The continuing decline in rural population has
put many of these small governments out of business. In
many regions they continue in an enfeebled and slightly
ridiculous condition.[12] While outliving their usefulness to a
technologically advanced society, their resistance to adversity
gives evidence that they provide satisfactions, both functional
and psychological, to a portion of the rural population.

---

[11]The development of *barrio* government under a Barrio Charter
Act of 1962 is a step toward the formalization of local government
within the towns. This does not indicate, however, a
movement toward the American pattern of proliferation.
[12]In several counties in Kansas at present (1965), there are
fewer than 100 persons for each unit of government. Other
states of the Great Plains can match this condition.

As has been pointed out, the presence of federal, state, and local governments operating in the same area with fairly loose interlocking relationships make possible a diversity of styles of government. The local township and rural school governments represent one pole of agrarian localism. Interrelationships are personal and equalitarian. The professional training of the rural school teacher is overcast with the behavioral requirements of rural society and mores.[13] The "functions" of the township are held firmly in the grip of farmers who give part-time service usually a few days a year, to township duties. The evidence indicates that loyalty to these little units of government is highest on the part of small farmers whose situation stems from as well as encourages an outlook of conservatism.

The tenacity with which the beneficiaries of small outmoded units cling to the status quo can be illustrated by the case of a struggle in one Kansas county to consolidate the township road systems into a county system.[14] In this case, one phase of economic development dealt with programs of efficiency and economy in local government. An appropriate committee produced detailed plans showing how to obtain the advantages of the county unit road system. At a meeting called for the purpose of adopting this proposal as a part of the development plan, however, it was summarily put to death. Among those appearing at the meeting were farmers employed part-time on township road maintenance. They simply produced a majority necessary for defeating the proposal. Conflict of interest apparently can be raised at humble as well as most sophisticated levels of government.

The difficulty of transferring functions from local to centralized units illustrated by the example above could be multiplied

---

[13]Everett M. Rogers, *Social Change in Rural Society* (New York: Appleton, Century, Crofts, 1960), pp. 239-41.

[14]Kansas Area Development Files, Kansas State University, Manhattan, Kansas. Kansas law is permissive on this matter, and by 1964 about half of the Kansas counties had adopted county unit road systems.

indefinitely. Proposals for centralizing schools have produced the same phenomenon throughout much of rural America. Usually the transfer of functions to a county unit is indicative of considerable centralization. Yet counties are themselves, in

TABLE 2. POPULATION GAIN OR LOSS, 1950–60, AS COMPARED TO
BUDGET INCREASE OR DECREASE, 1950–60, FOR UNITS OF
GOVERNMENT IN ONE COUNTY, NORTHWEST KANSAS*

	Population Change (in percent)	Budget Change (in percent)
Group I: Population loss and budget decrease		
Township A	− 34.1	− 8.5
CITY A	− 32.1	− 9.9
Township B	− 13.9	− 7.2
Township C	− 9.6	− 4.7
Township D	− .9	− 43.5
Group II: Population loss and budget increase		
Township E	− 37.3	+ 119.5
Township F	− 20.0	+ 16.2
CITY B	− 19.4	+ 32.4
Township G	− 17.1	+ 8.6
Township H	− 13.6	+ 23.2
CITY C	− 12.4	+ 297.8
Township I	− 8.9	+ 53.5
Township J	− 6.2	+ 19.4
County	− 2.8	+ 13.3
Township K	− 2.5	+ 12.8
CITY D	− 1.7	+ 26.5
Group III: Population gain and budget increase		
CITY E	+ 9.1	+ 119.0
Township L	+ 3.0	+ 77.8
Group IV: Population gain and budget decrease		
Township M	+ 1.2	− 2.7

*Budget figures used were estimated expenditures for both years.
1955 used as base year because 1950 figures were not available.

most cases, organized in a way that reflects much of the personal
and amateur rather than the impersonal and professional types
of government.

It is recognized that the classification of governmental
administration into amateur and professional corresponds very
imperfectly with rural and urban. Much urban government
has been amateur. However, a trend toward professionalization
of urban government services has characterized the twentieth
century.[15] The same trend can be discerned in rural government
if the local operation of federal field services is examined.
Agricultural field services are often operated with the size,
expertise, and impersonalism that delight the most up-to-date
votaries of public administration.

Rural local governments remain havens of conservatism even
after the per capita costs of this style of services reach fantastic
heights. Superficially it would seem more tenable that politically
conservative persons would view high-cost services as anathema.
Table 2 indicates how slight are the effects of rising per capita
costs and declining populations in inducing small units to
rationalize their operations through consolidation. In fact, the
data indicate that the most popular (11 of 19 units of
government) correlation between variables is the association of
population decrease with an increasing budget.

In rural America, county government is, in the main,
amateur government, notwithstanding the long tenure of some
officials. Professional elements of these governments are
generally little more than appendages, in the nature of
county engineers or agriculture experts, federal grant-in-aid
supported agents employed under central office standards and
performing duties calling for some technical or professional
competence. The boundary between rural and urban is a
matter of definition, but if anything approaching the census
definitions are employed, rural characteristics pervade many

---

[15]The theme of the well-known novel by Edwin O'Connor, *The
Last Hurrah,* dramatizes the change from personal dispensation of
political favors to bureaucratic professionalism in an urban setting.

urban county courthouses. A typical case would be the county government in a midwestern county seat of 40,000, where the total county population is perhaps 55,000. In such a setting, the county government is a bastion of rural life and interests. It is a means by which rural life and values are made a part of the civic virtue and are democratized and legitimized. Change comes slowly to the county court house, on both sides of the Mason-Dixon line.

THE STRUGGLE FOR REAPPORTIONMENT

Among the several sets of public institutions sharing responsibility for maintaining agrarianism and shaping its evolving content, the state legislatures have a particular importance. As urban areas increased in economic power after 1900 and urban problems pressed for attention, state legislatures remained attached to rural constituencies. It would have been difficult in any case to have kept legislative district boundaries in line with the rapidly changing population distribution; as revision lagged the will to change weakened and justification of area representation developed. Representation by counties or by districts, which began as a convenient way to represent people, came to be defended on its own merits—that counties as counties should be represented.[16]

Thus the legislatures of many states, even some far advanced in urbanization, continued to represent the farmers and villagers out of proportion to their numbers. Constitutional

---

[16]"Thomas Jefferson repeatedly denounced the inequality of representation provided for under the 1776 Virginia Constitution and frequently proposed changing the state constitution to provide that both houses be apportioned on the basis of population. In 1816 he wrote that 'a government is republican in proportion as every member composing it has his equal voice in the direction of concerns . . . by representatives chosen by himself. . . .' Letter to Samuel Kercheval, 10 Writings of Thomas Jefferson (Ford, ed., 1899) 38." Noted by C. J. Warren in *Reynolds* v. *Sims,* 377 U.S. 533, 573 *fn.* (1964). Malapportionment has been a characteristic of state legislatures from the beginning. By 1960 it had become virtually a universal characteristic, with rapidly growing suburban areas the most disadvantaged.

provisions for reapportionment, often mandatory
in appearance, were ignored over long periods. Kansas, with a
constitutional requirement for reapportionment every five
years, did not reapportion its senate for over fifty years,
while its lower house was limited by a constitutional maximum
of 125 members with at least one from each of the 105
counties. In 1960, Alabama had not reapportioned since
1900, despite a state constitutional requirement that the
legislature be reapportioned decennially. In Virginia,
with no express standards for proportional representation,
reapportionment was carried out, as required, at decennial
intervals. But, under the 1962 law, the population per state
senator varied from 61,730 to 102,930, while in the lower
house representation varied as much as 4.36 : 1. In the
United States the lag in reapportionment by 1960 made it
possible in twenty-four states for less than 30 percent of the
population to elect a majority of the members of the
upper house of the legislature; the same was true with respect
to the lower house in fourteen states.[17]

That reapportionment should be withheld from the arena
of controversy as late as the 1960's can be attributed to
the high regard for rural values. The American people
shrank from changes that would legitimize urban control over
state legislatures. In addition, some of the necessary public
policies for urbanizing societies could be managed through
such devices as metropolitan home-rule or by federal subventions.

The findings of Derge, that a sharp rural-urban conflict
appears very infrequently in roll-call votes in Missouri and
Illinois legislatures, substantiates the thesis that American
cities are infiltrated with agrarian values and also have within
themselves sufficient intergroup conflict to blur the rural-urban
division.[18] State government legislative policies have tended to

---

[17]Glendon Schubert, *Reapportionment* (New York: Charles
Scribner's Sons, 1965), pp. 80–82.
[18]David R. Derge, "Metropolitan and Outstate Alignments in
Illinois and Missouri Legislative Delegations," *American
Political Science Review* (December 1958), 1065.

be oriented toward rural and agricultural interests while urban
needs have occupied a lower priority for attention and action.[19]
Grants to local schools and other units, state road-building
programs, and policies of the archaic units of rural local
government discussed above, are slanted toward and have
generally been successful in providing significant advantages
to agriculturists. Although the differences between urban
and rural or metropolitan and rural are not evidenced
in roll-call votes in state legislatures, Grumm found a
significant difference in voting in the state legislature in
Kansas when the variable was economic growth. That is,
representation from areas that evinced positive growth responded
in a significantly different fashion on roll-call votes from
representatives whose districts were declining economically.[20]

The factor of economic decline injects another variable
into the discussion, one that cannot be treated in this section.
However, there can be little doubt that a part of the civic
outlook of agrarians of the present day is a result of the
difficulties and conflicts that are concomitants of the
technological revolution in agricultural production. Evidence at
hand shows that rural areas and villages near cities participate
in economic growth and development like that of the city
while rural areas not in a proximate relationship to a city
or cities are most likely to decline in population, trade, and
business. The anxiety generated by economic decline has
generated conservative policies in terms of private investments
and at the same time has fostered policies regarding public
programs that are viewed as liberal. The latter are public
improvement or state-federal subsidy programs concerning
which a favorable state legislature can be helpful. Hence,
a rationale has emerged for a community of interests between
the small and amateur local governments and the rustic state

---

[19]William C. Havard and Loren P. Beth, *The Politics of
Misrepresentation: Rural-Urban Conflict in the Florida
Legislature* (Baton Rouge: Louisiana State University Press, 1962).
[20]John Grumm, "A Factor Analysis of Legislative Behavior," *Midwest
Journal of Political Science* (November 1963), 336–56.

legislators which does credit to the political perspicacity of the agrarian. This element of the rural gerrymander is not dealt with in most of the literature on the subject which pursues the matter normatively, usually with condemnation. It is, furthermore, no surprise that Derge's research does not turn up the real lines of conflict while Grumm's does, although incompletely.

The relationship between reapportionment and agrarianism is more clearly reflected in the reactions to the Supreme Court's opinions than in the opinions themselves. Following March 26, 1962, when *Baker* v. *Carr* (369 U.S. 186) was handed down, the Supreme Court resolutely set about redressing state legislative malapportionment.[21] Though the facts varied somewhat from state to state, the essence of the opinions and the structure of the arguments were similar. Almost always there was a long history of increasing malapportionment, sometimes accomplished by legislative refusal to heed a constitutional mandate to reapportion. Then it has been necessary to rebut the federal analogy—that the equal state representation in the United States Senate provides an appropriate model for one house of state legislatures. This rebuttal is effected by pointing out the fact that local units of government are made by and are subject to the discretion of the states in which they are located— as the states are not respecting the national government.

The Fourteenth Amendment to the federal constitution provided the standard against which the state legislatures were measured. As the Supreme Court said in *Reynolds* v. *Sims,* speaking through Chief Justice Warren:

A citizen, a qualified voter, is no more nor no less so because he lives in the city or on the farm. This is the clear and strong

---

[21]Representative opinions include *Scholle* v. *Hare,* 369 U.S. 429–435; *Reynolds* v. *Sims,* 377 U.S. 533–631; *WMCA* v. *Lomenzo,* 377 U.S. 633–655; *Maryland Committee for Fair Representation* v. *Tawes,* 377 U.S. 656–677; *Davis* v. *Mann,* 377 U.S. 678–694; *Lucas* v. *Forty-Fourth General Assembly of the State of Colorado,* 377 U.S. 713–765.

command of our Constitution's Equal Protection clause. This is
an essential part of the concept of a government of laws and
not men. . . . The Equal Protection Clause demands no less
than substantially equal states legislative representation for all
citizens, of all places as well as of all races.[22]

The impact of the new judicial attitude was widespread.
Of the fifty states, thirty-nine were involved by 1964 in
litigation on the question of legislative representation.
Generally, state legislatures had been responsible for
reapportioning themselves. The ease with which they
rationalized the widening inequality underscores a willingness
to classify city ways of life as something separate—an
exception to the accepted equalitarian culture. In this way,
the rural parts of government, the local units and counties,
and the state legislatures acted in such a way as to exclude
urban life and problems.[23]

The intensity of feeling about the question of reapportionment
is revealed by the unpopularity of the Supreme Court and
its Chief Justice after 1962. What the school-segregation case
accomplished in 1954 to inflame anti-court feelings
in the South, the reapportionment cases did in and after
1962 throughout the land. After these latter decisions,
"Impeach Earl Warren" posters appeared along
highways of the Midwest. Country weeklies editorialized
vigorously against the Court, finding its rulings a part
of the general conspiracy in Washington for a
"federal take-over."[24] It is ventured that the groups

---

[22]*Reynolds* v. *Sims,* 377 U.S. 568.
[23]In most states, the organization of political parties has followed
the legislative pattern. A question whose answer reveals much
about the state party is the extent to which it is dominated
by rural leadership.
[24]An example of the circuitous reasoning of country editors is
found in the *Lyons Daily News* (Lyons, Kansas), May 5,
1965. Pushing the federal analogy to its limit, the editor
opined that: "There is much to quarrel with in the move to
reapportion the (Kansas) House of Representatives. Territories
deserve representative bodies in government for protection
and balance in governing judgment. . . .
"Maybe the move here in Kansas is a prelude to reapportionment

on the "far right wing" in American politics drew much
added strength from rural America as a result of the
reapportionment decisions of the Court.

THE FEDERAL ARENA OF FARM POLITICS

The preceding excursion into local and state agrarian
politics was not intended to displace consideration of the
federal government's role in agriculture; it was included to
provide a more complete framework for understanding the
institutional embodiment of agrarianism in public affairs.
The strong expression of the ideology that is found
in traditional rural government and rural-oriented state
legislatures is much too important to overlook; the behavior
of these institutions provides a key to understanding that is
not easily gleaned from observations of policy-making
at the federal level.

Figure II illustrates the ideological relationships in
a general way (no attempt is made at a scale of precise

FIGURE II.   TRADITIONAL AGRARIANISM AND MODERNIZATION
IN TWO SETS OF PUBLIC INSTITUTIONS

Rural Local Government and Rural State Legislatures	*National Bureaucracy (Including Congress) Metropolitics*
TRADITIONAL AND FUNDAMENTAL AGRARIANISM	Traditional and Fundamental Agarianism
	MODERNIZED INSTITUTIONS AND CORRESPONDING POLICY EXPRESSIONS
Modernized Institutions and Corresponding Policy Expressions	

at the national level. . . . One wonders when the Supreme
Court will find the Constitution unconstitutional."

proportions). In little rural governments and unreformed state legislatures expressions of traditional and fundamental agrarianism are dominant, behavior tends to match the expressions, and the riches and the poverty of this philosophy are abundant. The federal agricultural bureaucracy and the national Congress express, dominantly, a "modernized agrarianism." A subordinate theme of traditional agrarianism can be identified, somewhat muted, however, and no longer likely to have the confident majoritarian tone that prevailed from Jefferson to Bryan. This sector of agriculture has been too long engaged in a rear-guard action.

The federal government's role in agriculture has been subjected to extensive study from various perspectives, particularly that of economics.[25] Through the years this role has become increasingly impressive, conspicuous, and controversial, a development most marked in the ongoing and expanding commercial farm programs stemming from the New Deal of the 1930's.

These programs can be seen in retrospect as extensions of earlier policies which had their origins in classical agrarianism blended with fundamentalism. The nineteenth-century federal land policy was combined with the democratic ethic in such legislation as the Morrill Act of 1862, the Experiment Station Act of 1887, the Reclamation Act of 1902, and the Extension Service Act of 1914. All of these resulted in federal, regional, or state field services of considerable scope. At a time when private commercial and industrial interests were probing the economy and gaining centralized control over its development, government—federal, state, local—was controlled or thought to be controlled by

---

[25]Examples are Harold G. Halcrow, *Agricultural Policy of the United States* (Englewood Cliffs: Prentice-Hall, 1953); Dale Hathaway, *Government and Agriculture: Economic Policy in a Democratic Society* (New York: Macmillan, 1963); Rainer Schikele, *Agricultural Policy* (New York: McGraw-Hill, 1954); Murray R. Benedict, *Farm Policies of the United States, 1790-1954: A Study of Their Origins and Development* (New York: Twentieth Century Fund, 1953).

these private groups. Contemporarily with this development, federal field activities were, through state or local outlets, serving agriculture. On the one hand, government was limited; on the other hand, government services were extended. And extension of services had the agricultural interests as a central focus.

The truly remarkable nature of these pre-New Deal federal agencies is more apparent when the generally restrictive nature of the federal government of that time is considered. With the change of the general public philosophy into that characterized as the New Deal, it could easily be foreseen that the federal agricultural establishment would grow apace. This has happened.

The view taken here is that the dynamics of American agrarianism find a distinct expression through public institutions. This public side of American agrarianism is channeled into two sets of institutions, each of which responds to a sector of the complex whole making up the agricultural community. More accurately, both sectors receive political inputs from the total community but the dominant roles are reversed, as indicated by Figure II. One sector, the traditional, has found expression in the familiar local institutions of rural government and in state legislatures; the other, the rational sector, is represented by federal agriculture policy. This view regards the totality of public institutions related to agrarianism as a system, the parts of which are in some respects complementary. The total public system reflects agrarianism with varying degrees of intensity; the ideology, at the same time, has been reshaped by the empirical requirements of institutional survival.

Agrarianism in Congress

The American Congress serves admirably to reflect the tensions produced by conflicting interests within the electorate. A survey of the debates and hearings on farm issues makes it clear that there is a deep cleavage within the agricultural community. In the usual terms of reference, there is not one farm problem, but many. To resolve one may intensify others. A focus on one aspect of policy, such as price supports for basic farm products, may enhance the likelihood of neglect of problems confronting other sectors of the society.

The way in which the enterprise-production value dominated the policy objective at the national level is a well-documented record. Inescapably, the major farm legislation after 1920 has shown a consistent solicitude for the commercial farmer. The thrust of political power for favorable federal policies in price, credit, and production policies has been strengthened by the leading farm organization, the American Farm Bureau Federation. By the same token, these forces successfully opposed the development of policies giving more than minor consideration to alleviating some serious socioeconomic problems, such as conditions of migrant workers, underemployment in rural areas, and deterioration of rural institutions.

The pressure of the major farm organization was further augmented, not only by special commodity interest groups, but even more by the agricultural educational and research establishments. These latter have established the standards for successful agricultural life in terms which are unattainable by traditional agrarians and the rural poor. In this context, one perceptive observer notes that

With the major cleavages in agriculture now channeled in partisan directions, the position of the Farm Bureau as the source of policy has been challenged but not overcome. The dominant farm spokesmen have veered toward the ideological perspectives of the industrialism they originally sought to combat. . . . If there is to be a change, it will have to come from those who control the expression of agrarian belief . . . the conservatism of the leaders has remained intact.[26]

While the political partisanship referred to above is discernible, it is one of the least precise measures for

---

[26]Harmon Zeigler, *Interest Groups in American Society* (Englewood Cliffs: Prentice-Hall, 1964) pp. 197–98.

differentiating among the various cleavages within agriculture.
In partisan politics, a strong tendency toward independence
remains alive among agrarians. Even the party labels
worn often acquire a regional substance. North Dakota
Republican candidates have positions that would win
few Republican votes outside that state. In the aggregate,
however, a rough congruence appears between the Farm
Bureau, rural Republicans and southern Democrats, conservatism,
and land-grant institutions. A less orderly community of
interests at the other side of the spectrum would consist
of the Farmers Union, northern rural and urban Democrats,
marginal and traditional farmers, and labor. Unattached
with any firmness to either of these communities are many
of the rural poor, migrants, minority races, share-tenants, and
nonmobile rural labor. Not all of the unattached are
economically deprived, but most of them are.

How does Congress mirror the agrarian ideology? What
values does it depict that are not represented in rural-dominated
state legislatures or in little rural governments?

As continuation of the legislative policy of price support
for basic crops inaugurated in the 1930's had become
conservative policy by 1960, with some marginal exceptions,
legislation was conceived to cope with the farm problems along
lines broader than production in basic crops. This line of
policy took many forms, some reaching back to early years of
the New Deal and sometimes attaining the level of
action programs.[27]

Some of the most revealing measures, in terms of expressed
ideology, are those that attempt to revitalize "areas," or
communities, with recognition that such a process may require
major socioeconomic changes. Such a measure was the

---

[27]One of the best examples of this type of legislation was the
Farm Security Act, resulting in the Farm Security Administration.
The tribulations of this program at the hands of the agricultural
power elite are narrated in Grant McConnell, *The Decline of
Agrarian Democracy* (Berkeley: University of California Press,
1953).

Tennessee Valley Authority Act of 1933, a historic landmark both in achievement and in controversy. Another may well be the Appalachia Redevelopment Act of 1965, whose fate is yet to be unfolded in programmatic terms. Because these measures strike at the heart of the rural problem, overriding class and conventional niceties with unorthodox tools, they are less likely to be accepted as means of resolving the "farm problem" than such legislation as the Soil-Bank plans or the Feed Grains Acts.

The Area Development Model

In like manner, the consideration of the Area Redevelopment Acts of the late 1950's and early 1960's brought out many facets of the agrarian struggle. The Department of Agriculture published a report in 1955, "The Development of Agriculture's Human Resources, A Report on Problems of Low-Income Farmers," which documented the extent of poverty in the low-income agricultural group.

President Eisenhower's solution to this problem proposed expansion of the agricultural cooperative extension service in order to give technical assistance to low-income rural counties. This was the approach that could be anticipated from a cautious Republican administration; it accepted the objective of raising the level of commercial activity or economic solvency of farmers. President Eisenhower's message recommended (1) improving production and marketing by the low-income farmers, (2) finding part-time off-the-farm jobs, and (3) appealing to states and counties to provide local support.

These recommendations were enacted by Congress, finally becoming law as an amendment to the Smith-Lever (Extension Service) Act on August 11, 1955. The law reflected the prevailing faith in commercial agriculture as the ideal agrarian way of life. The main function of the government with respect to the 1.5 million farmers whose incomes were below $1,000 per year in 1955 was to (1) counsel with them in local groups in appraising their capabilities to improve, (2) cooperate with other agencies in furnishing information about employment opportunities, and (3) provide information, advice, and counsel to farm families deciding to seek a new farming venture. It can be understood why Senator Douglas of Illinois, representing a more forceful approach to the problem, caustically labeled the administration (Eisenhower) measure "a conversation bill."

The record of hearings on this measure is illuminated by an exchange between the Administrator of the Federal Extension Service, Clarence M. Ferguson, and Representative Henry Aldous Dixon of Utah. In response to a statement by Administrator Ferguson that the Extension Service had been criticized, perhaps justly, for spending much time with well-to-do farmers, Representative Dixon asked if there was any direct financial aid to the farmer himself in the bill. To Mr. Ferguson's negative reply, the representative said: "I wish to commend it; I think it is one of the finest ideas that I have ever seen to help the low-income farmers."[28]

The sensitivity of Congress to the agrarian ethic of the twentieth century is reflected by such statements as that of Representative John Henderson of the Fifteenth District of Ohio, in which were located two "pilot" counties under the rural development program. He was sure inequalities could not be erased by handouts from the federal government because they would only create attitudes on the part of recipients "which would do anything but inspire ambition and desire to succeed." Furthermore, "American farmers are made of something more sturdy than that. They do not want handouts. They have traditionally been the business pioneers and examples of industry and hard work in this Nation."[29]

Plainly, the several pieces of legislation that went into the rural economic development during the 1950's point up the acute dilemma in agricultural policy. And it is a dilemma that

---

[28]U.S. Congress, House of Representatives, Committee on Agriculture, Hearings, Extension Service Appropriations, 84th Congress, First Session, 1955, p. 36.
[29]*U.S. Congressional Record,* 85th Congress, First Session, 1957, 105, Part 1, p. 328.

can be expressed in the terms of agrarian ideology. That is, given the myth of agrarianism, what policy can be developed that will provide for reducing the ills of American agriculture? Obviously, to maximize the equalitarian small-holder element of the myth is to forego the fundamentalism-successful business elements that have become the dominant themes of the ideology.

The public record suggests the following lines of development:

1. The large commercial farmer consistently retains the dominant voice in federal agriculture policy. Even so, his spokesmen consistently pay homage to the tradition of an older agrarianism by speaking of the need to preserve "the family farm." (*The Congressional Record,* 85th Congress, First Session, lists seven bills introduced in that session with the purpose "of strengthening the family farm" and of preserving the independence of agriculture.) Thus the classical agrarianism is perpetuated in symbolic or ceremonial form while fundamentalism is made a part of the working policy.

2. Those who would help the small farmer with more than "conversation" legislation are a minority. Yet they are heard and, given the pluralistic nature of congressional organization and procedure, are not entirely ineffective. Their successes are mostly short-run and admittedly have never reached to the roots of the deepening blight of rural poverty.

3. The agrarian ideology has evolved with changing socioeconomic conditions, and this evolution has brought tensions and contradictions within the rural population. These complications have tended to encourage manifold expressions of the agrarian ideology. An expressive function of government, distinct from the instrumental, is indicated.

4. The evidence indicates that the federal programs have not alleviated the problems of American rural society, although in numerous cases commercial farms have been kept solvent by them. On the contrary, the blight of rural areas has steadily increased.

A bill introduced in the 85th Congress by Senator Douglas

designed to provide direct help to such areas gave rise
to much the same kind of debate. Senator Cotton of
New Hampshire did not like "the long arm of the federal
government reaching into an area." Area development, though
apparently a suitable matter of conversation, was not "a
legitimate province of the federal government." To Mr. Alger
of Texas the bill was fantastic, socialistic, an abdication of
state's rights, and a repudiation of the Constitution.
Representative Knutson, on the other side, defended the
stronger Douglas bill, noting the need to bring rural people to
the level of urban community income. Though the record
held convincing evidence, she saw no need to go into bitter
details about farm families forced off the farm and thousands
trying to make a living under present circumstances without
money to repair equipment, struck by disasters and without
disaster relief. As Representative Brown of Missouri saw it:
"Nothing is worse than seeing plain God-fearing country
folks unable to make a living on the family farm, forced
to leave their lifelong homes and neighbors to go looking for
work in strange and distant cities where they do not choose to
live. This is cruel."[30] The bill passed Congress but was
pocket-vetoed by President Eisenhower.

Area Development: Rural or Urban

The conviction persists that unemployment is an urban
problem, not rural. When President-elect John F. Kennedy's
task force on distressed areas reported to him on December
29, 1960, it included 300 to 400 rural or small-urban areas.
Its recommendations, however, did not follow the usual rural
norms of rescuing one-family commercial farms by farming
improvements. They were urban-like in tone, suggesting
unemployment compensation, public works, general assistance,
federal procurement (defense contracts), and similar

---

[30]*U.S. Congressional Record,* 85th Congress, Second Session, 1956,
104, Part 14, p. 17,900.

measures. A bill incorporating these items was introduced by Senator Douglas, who emphasized the problem of rural underemployment.

Opponents of this measure were critical of such an approach. To them it seemed questionable to take the problem of unemployment out of its urban context. They also doubted that business enterprises could be attracted away from the cities. Finally, Representative Meader doubted that depressed areas should be "exploited to promote socialism, which actually will harm instead of helping them . . . this bill should be called a bill to socialize the American economy by federal intrusion into the equity end of enterprises; to assist in pirating the same through politics . . . and for other socialistic purposes."

Rural area development in the 60's became inextricably involved with urban-type problems and goals. Many of the physical elements of the environment are urban in nature. Many rural dwellers can by airplane or freeway arrive at the heart of a metropolis as quickly as a suburbanite can reach the same destination in ordinary traffic. Yet policy makers see the rural problem in a specialized category. Paradoxically the agrarian is at the same time superior and inferior to the urbanite. The city is both an attraction and a repellant.

Development on an area or a regional basis is a national responsibility. Yet national programs, caught up in the agrarian ideology, are frequently transferred to the state, a level of governmental action preferred by agrarians.[31] If such a program is administered at the federal level, the preferred agency is the Agricultural Cooperative Extension Service, in whose hands agrarian values are thought safe.

---

[31]Harry M. Caudill, "Misdeal in Appalachia," *Atlantic Monthly*, 215 (June 1965), pp. 43-48.

5

SOCIAL CONTEXTS
OF
AMERICAN
AGRICULTURE

We here examine agrarian ideology in two contexts: on the one hand, as it was articulated in the years 1872–1918 by advocates who spoke to or wrote for farmers who lived in different milieus; on the other, as it is expressed by present-day respondents who represent different degrees of involvement with or proximity to agriculture.

The first thesis to be examined assumes that city and country in America became implicated in a common system during the nineteenth century. Within this context we argue that farmers residing closer to cities attributed a different quality to the city than did those who resided a greater distance from cities. The descriptions of farming, the rural community, and the city published in the annual reports of the State Board of Agriculture of Kansas and Massachusetts will be used to test this thesis.

These sources of data also allow agrarianism to be observed in the time between the Civil War and World War I, when ascendant industrialization impacted the farm community. Farmers and their advocates wrestled with the trend to industrialization and wrested some tribute from the public in the era. The period's dynamism is manifested in that American agriculture experienced a zenith and a nadir in this half-century.

Present-day agriculture as a segment of modern American society is examined by means of interviews and demographic data. The context of the analyses is provided by two questions: How does agrarianism relate to modern agriculture? What are the present consequences of the social differentiation that has been occurring in the farm community? Answering the latter question resulted in proposing a new conceptual view of the differentiated occupation of farming. Interviews were conducted in four groups of counties of Kansas. Four classes of respondents were enumerated. Two classes, randomly chosen to represent residents of towns and cities and general farmers, had a more or less direct connection with agriculture. Also, respondents termed "outstanding" farmers were interviewed. They had been nominated by knowledgeable persons as manifesting the best managerial attributes in farming. Several residents in their communities recognized that the extent to which they applied scientific agricultural practices and the incomes they realized from farming set them apart from farmers in general. Purposive sampling was practiced within this list of nominees to insure that the kinds of agricultural enterprises followed in the area would be represented.[1] Outstanding farmers represented the category that others have identified as rational, progressive, businesslike.

The fourth class of respondents were students in residence at Kansas State University. All students who had entered the University from the surveyed counties of Kansas were

---

[1] In some areas a typical farm combined irrigated and nonirrigated enterprises. If a nominee followed only one of these enterprise systems, he was excluded from consideration because his farm did not represent the locale.

included. The inclusion of a student sample provided
expressions toward farming by respondents who had taken one
step away from their home community. Because the context
of agriculture about which respondents were questioned
concerned migration from farm areas, preferences from
persons who were temporary or permanent migrants
were meaningful.

Thus, the data collected were obtained from respondents who
have related differently to agriculture. On the one hand,
the written historical expressions of advocates of agriculture
were views grounded in the farm community. The articulators
described farming as special pleaders, representatives,
evangelists, or in other roles. Their key characteristic
for present purposes concerned their self-acknowledged
implication in farming as farmers or as occupational kin to
farmers. On the other hand, the survey in present-day agriculture
collected expressions from a broader range of respondents. Some
were implicated with farming, some had left agriculture, and
some were tangentially related to the industry.

Lastly, demographic data are utilized to describe the details
of the "two agricultures" of present-day America. The gross
contrast betwen these varieties of farming render them two
different social universes. Hence the two agricultures are
identified by terms which emphasize their distinctions. The
ideology of agrarianism provided the over-arching mantle under
which historical and contemporary evidence was analyzed.

IDEOLOGICAL EXPRESSION IN KANSAS AND MASSACHUSETTS

To analyze the expression of agrarianism, the annual reports
of the State Boards of Agriculture of Kansas and Massachusetts
were used for the periods of 1872–1894 and 1895–1918. The
earlier terminal date is used because this was the initiation of
the first annual report of the Kansas Board. The last terminal
date was dictated by a change of format of the Massachusetts
report. The mid-point coincides with the peak of Populism, a
movement that had grown as agricultural distress and depression

accumulated. Following the mid-point, the agricultural economy improved generally through World War I. The periods observed differ markedly. Much of the first period was characterized by discontent, and relative farm contentment characterized the second.

Demographic data indicate the changing secular balance between agriculture and other sectors of the economy.[2] Truesdell's data indicate that whereas nearly one-half (49.4 percent) of the nation's work force was in agriculture in 1880, its fraction, as reported in the *Census of Population,* had diminished to 1 worker in 15 by 1960. (See Table 3.) Although the agricultural work force increased numerically to World War I, it has experienced a numerical decrease in each period since then. On the other hand, nonagricultural workers

TABLE 3.   WORKERS IN AGRICULTURE AND NONAGRICULTURE
IN THE UNITED STATES, 1880–1960*

Decennial Census	All gainful workers	Workers in nonagriculture	Workers in agriculture	Percent of total in agriculture
1880	17,392,099	8,807,288	8,584,811	49.4
1890	23,318,183	13,957,253	9,360,930	40.1
1900	29,073,233	18,160,311	10,912,922	37.5
1910	37,370,794	25,779,141	11,591,653	31.0
1920	42,433,215	30,984,532	11,448,683	27.0
1930	48,829,920	38,357,922	10,471,998	21.4
1940	49,492,552	40,742,857	8,749,695	17.7
1950	58,998,943	51,985,118	7,013,825	11.9
1960	64,639,247	60,382,513	4,256,734	6.6

*Sources: Leon E. Truesdell, *Farm Population: 1880–1950,* Technical Paper No. 3 (Washington: Bureau of the Census, 1960), Table 1, p. 6; *U.S. Census of Population: 1960, General Social and Economic Characteristics* (Washington: U.S. Government Printing Office, 1961), PC (1)-1C, Table 92, p. 223.

[2] Leon E. Truesdell, *Farm Population: 1880-1950,* Technical Paper No. 3 (Washington: Bureau of the Census, 1960), Table 1, p. 6.

have increased from each year of observation to the next
throughout the eighty years. Rapid numerical growth in the
nonagricultural segment has accompanied numerical stability
or decline in number of farmers. In approximately three
generations the number outside of agriculture septupled.
Moreover, observing each intercensal period provides an
additional dimension of the changing agricultural work force.
(See Table 4.) Except for the second observed decade, the

TABLE 4.   PERCENTAGE CHANGE IN THE NUMBER OF WORKERS IN
          AGRICULTURE BETWEEN CENSUSES, 1880–1960

1880-90	1890-1900	1900-10	1910-20	1920-30	1930-40	1940-50	1950-60
+9.0	+16.6	+6.2	−1.2	−8.5	−16.4	−19.8	−39.3

general trend has been that the agricultural work force has
decreased at an increasing rate.

Approximately 8 percent of the Massachusetts and 60 percent
of the Kansas work force were occupied in agriculture in
1890.[3] Steady declines have occurred in each state since then.
Thus, in 1960 approximately one percent of the Massachusetts
labor force was employed in agriculture and 13 percent of all
Kansans were so occupied.[4] Throughout this period the
figure for the United States as a whole was intermediate between
the states. It was as late as the 1950's when the United States
occupational structure became as nonfarm-based as Massachusetts
had been in 1890. Moreover, Kansas' proportion of workers
in agriculture in 1960 (13.3 percent) substantially exceeded
the Massachusetts percentage (7.8 percent) of 1890. The states
represented, and represent, vastly different universes in their
farm-nonfarm mixes.

[3]*Ibid.*, Table 2, p. 18.
[4]*U.S. Census of Population, 1960; General Social and Economic
Characteristics* (Washington: U.S. Government Printing Office,
1961), PC(1), 18C (Kansas), 23C (Massachusetts), Table 62.

Some dimensions of difference were patently based in economic, political, and social conditions. During the last decades of the nineteenth century, Kansans were engaged in occupying virgin lands and creating the social fabric to meet collective needs. The frontier was not only physical and geographical but it was social as well. Eastern farmers of this era were legatees of mined agricultural resources and of a comparatively well-developed social environment within the farm community. Western farmers were acquiring or building that which eastern farmers had already built or consumed.

The generalized environments depicted provide a context for addresses and articles published by the Boards of Agriculture.[5] One general theme—farmers as victims—that may have been a derivative from the lack of fulfillment of agrarianism, had much greater relevance in the earlier period than in the later. (See Table 5.) However, the ways farmers were victimized were differently stated in the two sets of reports. Whereas Kansas authors expressing this theme cited the "robbery of agriculture," lamented the "extremity of suffering" of farmers, and vented their emotions on the classic oppressors of farmers— merchants, bankers, tax systems—as the causative agents of farm distress, in the Massachusetts reports expressions were directed against the "tuberculosis commissioner," or "City Boards of Health," or the "multiplicity of inspectors." In Massachusetts, public agencies scrutinized production methods on nearby farms to enforce sanitary practices. Representatives of consumers

---

[5]Many items solely concerned production problems of farmers. These were surveyed to determine the incidence of references to agrarianism, the city and rural community, and other subjects that concerned us. Subjects which were more fruitful were those specified above as well as those concerned with organizing farmers, rural schools and churches, and other rural institutions. Published discussions of lectures were also included. The annual reports of the Secretary of the Board, of the Overseers of the Massachusetts Agricultural College, of the Agricultural Experiment Station, of the several crop or livestock commissions or boards, were not read. The Kansas reports also published verbatim copies of articles or editorials that had appeared elsewhere. When the latter fell within the limits prescribed above, they were analyzed.

TABLE 5. THEMES EXPRESSED IN SELECTED ARTICLES AND
ADDRESSES PUBLISHED IN ANNUAL REPORTS OF THE
STATE BOARD OF AGRICULTURE OF KANSAS AND
MASSACHUSETTS: PERCENTAGE DISTRIBUTIONS

	1872–1894		1895–1918	
Themes Expressed	*Kansas*	*Mass.*	*Kansas*	*Mass.*
AGRARIAN	10.7	23.5	17.1	16.5
Independence	2.7	2.9	4.2	1.7
Fundamentalism	4.0	12.0	5.8	7.9
Moral virtues	4.0	8.6	7.1	6.9
FARMERS AS VICTIMS	18.7	7.3	8.5	4.8
NONAGRARIAN	70.6	69.2	74.5	78.6
Characteristics of farmers, farming	12.0	31.4	25.4	27.7
Organizations: farm or community	40.0	8.6	7.9	12.3
Education or schools	1.3	15.8	24.6	21.2
Negative to farm, positive to nonfarm	4.0	5.2	5.2	7.3
Farm-city migration	0.0	3.0	5.8	5.1
Other	13.3	5.2	5.6	5.0
Total percent	100.0	100.0	100.1	99.9
Number	(75)	(558)	(674)	(722)

intruded into farm enterprises. Farmers close to cities apparently
had to incorporate urban preferences and standards into their
farming operations.

Over-all, classical agrarian expressions received minor attention.
The notion of the independent farmer received least attention
within the agrarian ideology in each period and state. Perhaps
independence had been sufficiently undermined by the late
nineteenth century to receive only limited expression. Even in
the earlier period observed here, Massachusetts articles
extensively stressed the interdependence between farm and city.
The scale of attention to interdependence perhaps diminished
proportionally the extent to which independence could
be articulated.

The other portions of the agrarian ideology, fundamentalism and the moral virtues of farming, received more attention. Between the observed periods, Kansas authors increased their attentiveness to these elements while the authors in Massachusetts decreased their attention relatively. Perhaps no testimony as to the fundamental quality of agriculture or the morally virtuous character of farmers is necessary when an area is wholly or predominantly agricultural. The ordering and acquisition of social eminence, the nature of social institutions, styles of living, and orientations of a homogeneous community constitute a culture that includes relatively few alternatives. There would be little disagreement as to the affective power of these elements in a farm community isolated from communities with other economic bases. Man's chief, perhaps sole, antagonist in this community is nature.

However, advocates of rural living who expressed their ideology in the shadow of the city could well magnify portions of it under circumstances in which attractive occupational or residential alternatives to farming were near at hand. Perhaps unequivocal disconfirmation of independence served to accent more powerfully the articulation of the moral and fundamental natures of farming. Moreover, disconfirmation of these elements was not so empirically accessible in view of the deluge of counter arguments. Hence, articles published in both sets of reports abounded with references to the morality of farmers as "creators," as followers of a "sacred" or "holy" occupation, and as having interests that could not be rendered in terms of "money alone." Also, it would have been impolitic to have strenuously opposed agricultural fundamentalism when so many published articles emphasized the following kinds of remarks: the farm is the "breeding place of brains"; farmers are the "flower of American citizenship"; "agriculture must be the basis for all prosperity"; and farm communities "insured government stability." Although contrary remarks were published, their incidence was less and a generally less strident tone was used.

The Massachusetts data show agrarian expression in the circumstance of the proximate city. Kansas data show agrarianism

as it confronted the ascendant urban-based economy. Kansans
turned from building farms, communities, and a rural social
organization to confront the seemingly omnipotent urban-
industrial form of organization. The relationship between farm
and city in the eastern United States had evolved through a
secular process in which costs of adjustments were amortized
over generations. Kansas farmers did not have the benefit of
distributing these costs over an extended period. Frontier farmers
of the late nineteenth century became implicated in the
industrialized economy concurrently as they broke the sod. The
Kansas experience would approximate that of numerous farmers
in nations that have undergone "forced draft industrialization."[6]
Whether the American farm community of the last century
was in the eastern or western part of the nation, the industrialized
economy bred man-made antagonists for farmers: the city and
the market were externally induced factors to which
farmers adjusted.

In each state and each period, the bulk of expressions were
devoted to nonagrarian subjects. Although the distributions
were highly dissimilar for the earlier period, the arrays of
themes expressed became less dissimilar in the later period.[7]
The principal reason for the dissimilarity, irrespective of
period, stemmed from the different penchants to depict farmers
as victims. For purposes of analyzing, in greater detail, similarities
and differences between the two periods, let us turn to the
specified nonagrarian themes that were articulated.

---

[6]Clark Kerr *et al., Industrialism and Industrial Man* (Cambridge:
Harvard University Press, 1960). The authors used this phrase
to depict industrialization as it is staged in a centrally controlled
polity and economy whose officials desire rapid development.
[7]The gross distributions of themes between Kansas and Massachusetts were compared statistically to determine differences or
similarities. Using the three classes of themes—agrarian, victim,
nonagrarian—for the two time periods, the following outcomes
were obtained: 1872–1894, X^2 of 14.67, $2df$, $p = .001$; 1895–
1918, X^2 of 7.75 $2df$, $p = .05$; each was a significantly different
distribution. The environments represented in the surveyed
reports of the two state boards of agriculture were significantly
different from these analyses.

The remarkable concentration of themes on organizing farmers is apparent in the Kansas reports of the earlier period. This period was punctuated by Granger, Alliances, and Populist activities in the West. The intensity and the range of feeling with respect to farm organizations is indicated in the following comments. Farmers must "combine to fix prices"; they required a "well-considered organization"; their present condition was partially due to their "failure to organize"; and they had to become skilled in the "art of selling and buying." Organization appeared to be a panacea-like means to be utilized for multiple ends. The birth, florescence, and death of farmer political organizations in the West manifested a seeking of purchase with the variety of forces that affected farming. The great range of forces called forth many short-lived attempts. Apparently for frontier farmers, organizations constituted a means of control over forces that had victimized them. Their deprivations would be reduced by organization. The classical agrarian notion of the independent farmer was eroded by farmers seeking to organize.

The Massachusetts reports differed from the Kansas accounts in the earlier period. Addresses published by the Massachusetts Board acknowledged, in past tense, the fruits of the Granger movement. Thus, the "Grange lifted farming" or it had "improved farming" and its activities had influenced legislation. The organization had been obtained and was in existence. One rural group had legitimacy in the eastern United States. Perhaps attachment to a single organization was sufficient because eastern farm areas had already made some adjustment to the city and the market. Consequently, the range of problems confronting these farmers was narrow compared with the westerners. The historical record manifestly indicates that the fickle attachment that characterized westerners' affiliations to organized protest was not replicated in the East.[8]

A higher degree of agreement between the states concerning the subject of organizations is characteristic of the later period.

---

[8]The "historical record" as used here refers to the conclusions of the farmer protest literature and not to our data alone.

Farm organizations continued to be regarded as contestants in the market place. However, new specific objectives were articulated for them as the agricultural economy improved: organizations were regarded as a means to encourage specialized farm production and also to standardize (quality control) marketed goods; organizations also were more widely acknowledged as giving a voice to the rural community and as useful in improving rural living. Undoubtedly, views like those expressed in the Country Life movement were being stated. It is also noteworthy that highly specified objectives for farm organizations had replaced the vague and ambiguous charges of another generation. The nature of expressions suggested that some farmers were beginning to resemble their adversaries of the industrialized economy.

Except for the Kansas reports of 1872–1894, the attention paid to two subjects—descriptions of farmers and farming and of educational institutions—accounted for nearly one-half of all the citations in the surveyed reports. In both periods, there was a notable tendency to describe farmers in an explicit normative-evaluative context: they were defined by reference to others. Farmers were related to some standard as "better than" or "worse than" other social categories or farmers of other times and places. Hence, American farmers were neither "serfs" nor "peasants"; there were no "class distinctions" in this rural community; contemporary farmers "had abandoned their fathers' methods" and New England farmers experienced "fewer privations than [did farmers] in the West." Those who regarded farmers as falling short of a standard used designations like the following: many "farmers are menial"; they "lack development" or the "mental horizons of farmers [are] confined to their livelihood"; they tended to be "slow thinking" or to have followed a "socially and intellectually sterile" calling.

The simultaneous expression of contradictory themes and the assessment of farm conditions by standards prevailing elsewhere suggest the following: The transition underway was drastic, substantive, indeed revolutionary; it was an objectively painful ordeal for numerous farmers; farmers, more than other categories of the population, were, in their own and their advocates' eyes, the sole victims of the transition (or they were the only large segment of the population that could articulate their distress and be indemnified for their stress).

The farmers who were required to make the transition had been reared with a different social view of the world.[9] They had inherited a view of farming that placed it in an esteemed and eminent, perhaps preeminent, position in the world. The Jeffersonian thesis had been expounded to them. However, numerous events of their adulthood rendered this inherited view invalid.[10] Farmers who successfully negotiated the shoals of the transition were not only able to comprehend the new forms and adjust to the urban-industrial world but some undoubtedly profited from the new arrangements.

The change that adult farmers had been compelled to negotiate must have been analogous to the adolescent stage in the individual's life cycle. However, the significant others that socialized the adult farmer to new social behaviors were impersonal distant forces rather than kin or known persons. Moreover, many American farmers must have approximated those experiences that adult immigrants to the United States had undergone. One general difference obtained, however: the latter sought the American opportunity while the former were involuntarily subjected to the trial of change.

Topics in the field of education received increasing attention between the periods in both series. Even in the earlier period, the land-grant college had been a suitable subject for discussion in Massachusetts. Other than unadorned mentions of these institutions, two general views were articulated vis-à-vis farmers and the new colleges. Some consideration was given

---

[9]We are not accounting in this comment for the many first-generation immigrant farmers who had settled on American land.
[10]Two publications have relevance for the ensuing discussion: Paul Bohannon, *Social Anthropology* (New York: Holt, Rinehart, and Winston, 1963); especially useful was the section on "detribalization" in the concluding chapter. Daniel Lerner with S. Pevsner, *The Passing of Traditional Society* (New York: Free Press, 1964); the authors note the range of tensions experienced by those persons who have known traditional and modernized social situations.

to the nature of the investment farmers held in these colleges. Hence, urban graduates of A. and M. colleges would "help agriculture" and these colleges were "of and for the tillers of the soil." Other speakers admonished farmers by noting that the "agricultural college does not receive the support it deserves" or reassured them that the "agricultural college is opposed to laziness" or suggested to the assembly that the "colleges are not good" or extolled farmers because "schools and universities [had been] founded by farmers." Apparently, the college had been such a recent innovation that its roles and missions had not been institutionalized.

A strong contrast between educational themes characterized the Kansas and Massachusetts reports in the later period. Kansas articles focused on the provision and circumstances of elementary education while Massachusetts authors continued to stress higher education. Kansans were still oriented toward developing local community services a generation following the initiation of the state's board of agriculture. Specific references to instructing immigrants or their children appeared in Massachusetts articles. The connection between education and social mobility and migration was recognized by authors published in each series. Complaints on this theme most frequently noted that schools trained young people to urban residence. Particularly the Massachusetts authors complained that nonfarm references and illustrations in textbooks were instrumental in distracting rural young people from their native places.

Two additional themes also received increasing attention between the two periods. These were migration between farm and city and expressions that were antagonistic to farmers or farming or were positive toward nonfarm arrangements. In each period, the aggregation of these themes yielded a greater amount of attention in Massachusetts than in Kansas. The city, which was somewhat an underlying theme to these subjects, was relevant in both states. However, Massachusetts authors considered the city a fitter subject.

The Massachusetts audience was informed that the migration from farms would be stemmed by retaining in farming the "brightest" young people, which would occur when "farm living improved." At an early date, rural life needed upgrading to compete with the nearby city. One author observed that eastern farm youth had "gone to the cities or the West." Those who went west were obstensibly attracted by farming opportunities. Hence, eastern farming was simultaneously subjected to the twin competition of cities and frontier agriculture.[11]

Massachusetts articles in the later period increased the elaboration of the thesis that eastern areas provided hands to develop western agriculture. However, more attention was paid to other themes; remarks that derogated farmers and/or positively promoted urban interest and remarks that noted city-country interdependence received greatest emphasis. Thus, the "city man should have clean milk" provided by farmers. They attributed responsibility to farmers for out-migration in that "parents drive the college boy from the farm." An implicit charge was leveled against farmers as they noted that "criticism of the [land-grant] colleges has come from farmers."

The notion of interdependence was explicated several ways. For example, it was noted that townspeople could join farm groups and farmers could join chambers of commerce. The mixture of farm and urban populations was observed in that urbanites owned farms or seasonally occupied rural residences. Arguments favorable to effecting "agreements between buyer and seller" and to bringing "producers and consumers together" acknowledged the merging of rural and urban interests. While Massachusetts authors were concerned with rural depopulation,

---

[11]Intra-agricultural competition is a contemporary circumstance of relevance to farmers. In the winter of 1965 Kansas livestock producers objected to an Appalachian Development effort directed toward increasing livestock production in Appalachia. The Kansas stockmen were antagonized by the use of federal funds to assist production in competition with existing areas of production. Eastern farmers, they felt, would be advantaged by being located closer to eastern consuming centers which import meat from other areas of the United States.

their tones were moderate or neutral; their articulation of rural
virtues did not preclude a similar attribution to nonfarm callings
as well.

Somewhat in contrast to the Massachusetts expressions, the
Kansas reports of 1895–1918 gave predominant attention to
interdependence, which was followed in incidence by the
need to rebuild rural communities. Concerning interdependence,
Kansas audiences were advised that they should not "array
farmers against the town," that the country would "develop
with the city," and that the improvement of rural schools
would be beneficial for "farm and nonfarm occupations." The
remarks were not noticeably different from those of the
Massachusetts reports. The urban investment in rural areas was
cast in fundamentalistic terms as one speaker noted that "the
city must help the farm or we shall all go down." Remarks
like "businessmen cooperate with [4-H] club work" and
"bankers aid farmers" not only manifested interdependence but
cast nonfarmers in a favorable light.

One wonders about the social circumstances of communities
that had been so recently built requiring renovation in their
second generation. Apparently, as Kraenzel has pointed out,
the farm communities of the Great Plains had been developed
in a boomer psychology in which organizations and institutions
suitable to a densely settled population were established.[12] A
basic factor in the overelaboration of organizations and services
was undoubtedly the farm population base that had resulted from
the preemption of 160-acre farm units.[13] In a word, western
rural communities that had come into being with the closing
of the land frontier had been "overbuilt." The initial overbuilt
nature of many Kansas rural communities perhaps represented
an optimum level for numerous observers. Those who addressed
themselves to seeking means whereby the trend underway

[12]Carl F. Kraenzel, *The Great Plains in Transition* (Norman: The
University of Oklahoma Press, 1955), p. 286.
[13]Everett E. Edwards, "American Agriculture: The First 300 Years,"
Farmers in a Changing World: Yearbook of Agriculture, 1940
(Washington: U.S. Government Printing Office, 1940), pp. 222–23.

would be reversed apparently had such an optimum in mind. Thus, "club work will keep boys and girls on the farm," the hopeful view expressed by one author, conceived of this recently initiated program as a means to render the rural community a more attractive place of residence.

In conclusion, similarities were evident between articles published in the two series of reports concerning agriculture in transition. Certain methods, orientations, trends, rationales, or conclusions were common to the states. Perhaps this shared quality reflected the pervasiveness of the urban-industrial impact and/or that the infrastructure of agriculture—the land-grant colleges, the federal and state departments of agriculture, *ad hoc* arrangements like the Country Life Commission, the general farm organizations, and related organizations—had begun to integrate agriculture nationally and relate agriculture to the urban-industrial segments.

However, it is proposed that the surveyed articles implied a different authorship for the deprived state of rural life and suggested different means to reduce the deprivation. Kansas authors tended to note that farmers had had deprivation visited on them and hence, they were not responsible for their deprived condition. Because they were not responsible for their condition it was reasonable that the public assist farmers through the transition. Massachusetts authors noted that many deprivations suffered by farmers resulted from their own actions, or more appropriately their inaction. These farmers were held to be responsible for their condition. The culture of unadaptable farmers was not congruent with an industrializing economy. As to amelioration of rural conditions, Kansas authors emphasized that reduction of deprivation would occur through changed arrangements or through the action of new organizations or agencies. To a much greater extent, Massachusetts authors saw the methods of amelioration as being in hand; the change required was that certain farmers ought to avail themselves of existing services. According to this view, the provision of services was adequate but a sector of the public was apathetic or not privy to the available services.

The illustrations from southern Maryland provided in the third chapter will be recalled. The complaint of several Massachusetts authors apparently would have been cogent more than a generation later in another agricultural area. This is evidence that a subsistence, nonmarket-oriented agriculture has persisted in rural America.

That the city had impacted agriculture appears to be clear. However, the impact had been deflected into divergent courses depending on the agricultural milieu from which the urban-industrial development was observed.

VIEWS TOWARD TWO VARIETIES OF PRESENT-DAY AGRICULTURE

While the historical records described agriculture in different social milieus, we turn now to analyze by comparison and contrast two varieties of agriculture that exist today. Kansas data, including interview materials and demographic information, provide focused observations in a small geographic area, and the regional and national sample data provide information of a general scope. One area within Kansas, represented by the state's nine southeastern counties, is broadly characteristic of farming in the Ozark-Appalachian Highlands or in the Lake States Cut-over region. (See Figure III.) Farms are small, afford part-time employment to their operators, and are low in capitalization. This region of Kansas was settled early in the state's history. It reached an early economic peak, based on railroading, manufacturing, and mining of coal, zinc, and lead, from which it has gradually descended.[14] Perhaps a similarity exists between today's agriculture in this part of

---

[14]Carroll D. Clark and Roy L. Roberts, *People of Kansas* (Topeka: The Kansas State Planning Board, 1936). These authors designated three subregions for the state. Their eastern subregion included the nine counties of southeastern Kansas as we designated them. Our western region included the twenty-four westernmost counties in the state, whereas the western subregion as delineated by Clark and Roberts included an additional two columns of fifteen counties, a total of thirty-nine counties. Their analysis of variation among the subregions of Kansas indicated long-standing economic, social, and demographic differences.

FIGURE III.   COUNTY OUTLINE MAP INDICATING SOUTHEASTERN
AND WESTERN AREAS OF KANSAS

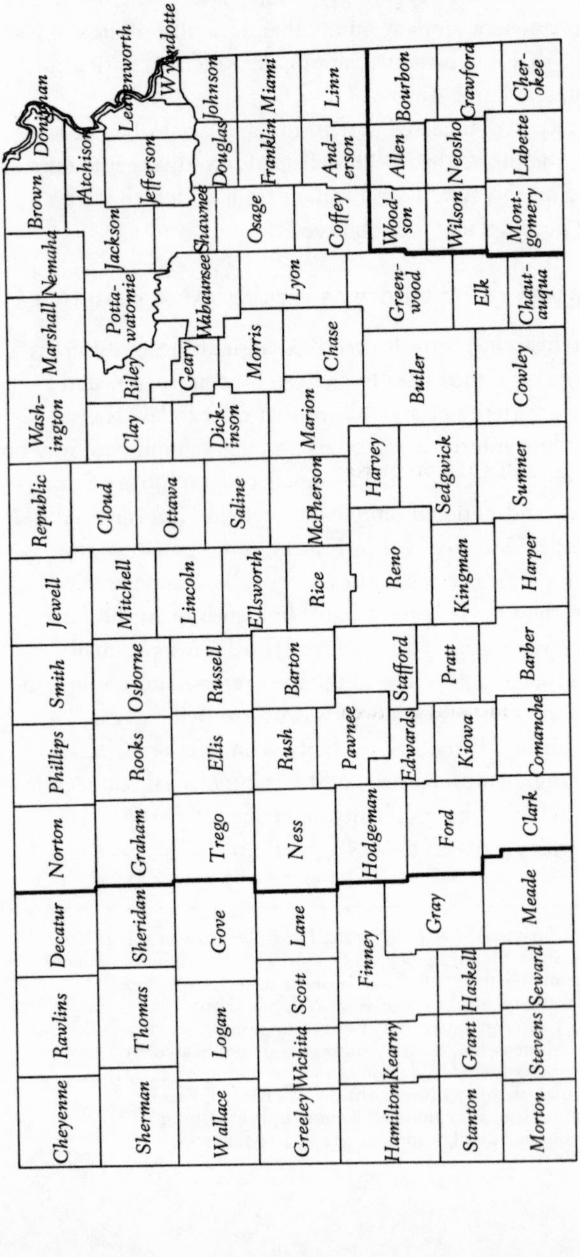

Kansas and the agriculture of Massachusetts in the early part of this century.

The twenty-four westernmost counties of Kansas constitute an agricultural economy. In local instances, extraction of oil or natural gas, regionally relevant small-scale manufacturing (much of it directly related to agriculture, according to our impressions), agriculturally related marketing or processing enterprises provide additional though limited alternatives. The region lies within the Great Plains. In this portion of the United States, cities are closely integrated with the agricultural industry.

The two regions are considered by reference to demographic variables in Table 6. Southeastern Kansas is much more densely settled than is western Kansas. In keeping with the density characteristic, far fewer western Kansans live in urban places and far more in small towns. Each area had a higher

TABLE 6.   DEMOGRAPHIC DATA FOR TWO AREAS OF KANSAS, 1960

Demographic Item	*Kansas*	*Nine counties of S.E. Kansas*		*Twenty-four counties of W. Kansas*	
		Range	*Median*	*Range*	*Median*
Persons per square mile	26.6	10.8–69.3	33.1	2.3–24.9	4.9
Percent of population in urban places (2500 or more)	56.5	65.7		35.5	
Percent of pop. in rural places (less than 2500)	18.0	13.5		29.0	
Percent of pop. outside of places	25.5	30.7		35.5	
Percent of pop., rural farm	14.7	10.0–41.8	21.1	4.3–55.4	30.8
Percent of employed males in agriculture (operator or wage labor)	17.8	8.7–41.7	20.0	7.3–66.0	45.9

average percentage of rural farm residents than did the state
Western Kansans were more dependent on agriculture as a
means of livelihood than were the Southeasterners. This was
true in 1960 and for the 1940 and 1950 censuses as well.
Reliance on agriculture was determined by the percentage of
employed males reported as farmers or farm laborers or foremen
in the censuses.

Whereas the demographic data indicated differences
between the regions, certain variables collected from the
Census of Agriculture (see Table 7) indicate that a mutually
exclusive character applies to the two parts of Kansas. The
three "value" items reported and degrees to which the farm
households relied on nonfarm income sources manifest
that significantly different economic arrangements apply
to farming in these regions. The average percentages reported
for farm operators working off their farms was close
to mutual exclusiveness. Moreover, the regions differed
substantially from the state's characteristics on several items.
Their ranging was toward opposite extremes from state
figures. With these observations in hand there can be little
dispute with the conceptualization that southeastern and
western Kansas represent varieties of farming.

The contemporary evidence we have employed involves
a different orientation from the historical evidence. The
referent in this section is agriculture; respondents represented
populations that related differently to agriculture.[15] The same
classes of respondents were surveyed in each region.[16]
Outstanding farmers had been designated as more successful
enterprisers than were their occupational fellows. College
students had come to the campus from the same areas in which

---

[15]The data utilized were collected from sampled populations in one
trade area of southeastern Kansas, centered on Chanute, and for
two trade centers—Colby and Garden City—for western Kansas.
Column headings of Table 8 specify the populations.
[16]Ralph E. Dakin *et al., Area Development: An Interdisciplinary
Approach to Research,* Bulletin 440 (Manhattan, Kansas: Agricultural Experiment Station, 1961). Area delineation and sampling
procedures are described on pages 10–13.

TABLE 7. DATA FROM THE CENSUS OF AGRICULTURE FOR TWO AREAS OF KANSAS

Demographic Item	Kansas	Nine Counties of Southeastern Kansas		Twenty-four Counties of Western Kansas	
		Range	Median	Range	Median
Percent commercial farms were of all farms, 1959	79.6	58.4–80.1	65.4	76.6–100.0	91.5
Percent of farm operators working off farms 100 days or more, 1959	23.8	22.0–41.1	27.6	9.3– 24.5	17.0
Percent of families whose other income exceeded value farm products sold, 1959	23.8	22.7–45.5	34.2	4.9– 20.3	11.5
Average dollar value farm products sold per farm, 1959	$10,667	$5,779–7,262	$5,963	$11,923–57,306	$21,342
Average dollar value farm products sold per farm, 1954	$6,670	$2,965–5,194	$3,627	$6,411–13,811	$10,123
Average dollar value of land and buildings, 1959	$57,233	$23,486–37,392	$31,807	$55,420–180,451	$107,330

TABLE 8. "IS MOVEMENT OF POPULATION AWAY FROM THE FARM BASICALLY DESIRABLE OR UNDESIRABLE?"
PERCENTAGE DISTRIBUTIONS OF RESPONSES FROM SOUTHEASTERN (1961) AND WESTERN KANSAS (1962)*

Movement from farms is:	Farm Residents				Nonfarm Residents			
	General		Outstanding		Householders		College students	
	South-eastern	West-ern	South-eastern	West-ern	South-eastern	West-ern	South-eastern	West-ern
Desirable	14.5	16.1	51.3	29.3	18.5	13.3	57.1	55.2
Undesirable	78.3	82.3	46.2	70.7	73.2	81.3	42.9	44.8
NA or NR	7.2	1.6	2.6	0.0	8.3	5.4	0.0	0.0
Total Percent	100.0	100.0	100.0	100.0	100.0	100.0	100.0	100.0
(Total Number)	(69)	(62)	(39)	(82)	(157)	(240)	(35)	(96)

*Chi square analyses were applied to respondents in the like samples for the regions. Thus, general farmers' responses were compared for southeastern and western Kansas. The following outcomes were obtained.: General—$X^2 = .0014$, 1 df, p of .95, significantly similar; Outstanding—$X^2 = 6.093$, 1 df, p of .02, significantly different; Householders—$X^2 = 2.346$, 1 df, p of .20, insignificant; College students—$X^2 = .038$, 1 df, p of .90, insignificant.

sampled householders resided.[17] The student sample allowed
us to observe responses from a population of persons actually
or potentially migrant. We held the premise that students
would view local agriculture in a different light from their elders.

Western Kansas was much more dependent than southeastern
Kansas on agriculture.[18] In fact, the pervasiveness of agriculture
essentially determines the fortunes of town or city residents.
On the other hand, the southeastern Kansas economy allowed
residents more choice of employment, although the range of
choice was being constricted through regional economic decline.

The compilations of data shown in Table 8 and computations
applied to them yielded the following observations:
irrespective of region, general farmers consider movement
from farms as undesirable. The similarity between these
general samples is a "real" similarity—chance as an
explanation for the similarity being reduced to 5 in 100.
However, region of residence yields a significantly different
response in observing outstanding farmers. Whereas western
farmers of this category designated migration from farms as
undesirable, a bare majority of the southeastern outstanding
farmers considered the movement desirable. It is observable,
however, that outstanding farmers, irrespective of region, were

---

[17]Areas delineated for interviewing farm, business, or household
samples yielded sufficient numbers of respondents in most
instances. For certain samples, in order to obtain a sufficient
number of respondents, we went beyond the bounds of the
delineated trade area into contiguous political jurisdictions. The
sampled college students were chosen by county of residence;
hence, they lived in the same counties as the householders
but some lived beyond the township of residence of sampled
householders.

[18]The last three censuses of the population indicate that the number
of males employed has declined by one-sixth in southeastern Kansas
and increased by nearly one-fourth in western Kansas. At the same
time, over-all declines have been registered for the number of
farmers and farm managers. However, the decrease was much
greater in the southeast, as compared to the west. Furthermore,
actual numerical increases were registered in western Kansas for
wage workers in agriculture. While the total employed labor force
declined in the southeast, agriculture declined more; while the
total increased in the west, agriculture declined.

more favorably disposed toward the movement of population
from farms areas than were general farmers.

Nonfarm householders, in approximately the same proportions
as general farmers, viewed the movement away from farm
areas as undesirable. However, the nonfarm samples
comprised of college students included more respondents
than any other category who stated that this was a desirable
move. There were regional differences between nonfarm
samples which had not been evident for farm samples.
Southeastern respondents, compared with western Kansas,
were much more likely to cite agrarian rationales as
buttressing the undesirability of the movement. (See Table 9).
And, although the data are sparse for the college sample,
fundamentalism was the theme most often cited in southeastern
Kansas. The argument western Kansas nonfarmers drew from
agrarianism echoes the choice—farmers as victims—that
was given by respondents who designated the movement as
desirable.

Farm respondents who regarded migration from farm areas
as undesirable were most likely to emphasize the moral
virtues of farming among the agrarian themes. In the
aggregate, the farm respondents articulated, in roughly
equal proportions, situations depicting farmers as having
been victimized or agriculture as having been the basic
industry. The theme of independence was cited so infrequently,
irrespective of sample, that it has perhaps lost its viability
as an agrarian element. At any rate, respondents who lived
in proximity to agriculture were not likely to characterize
farmers as independent.

Few of the respondents who designated movement from
farms as desirable (see Table 10) utilized agrarian themes
to elaborate on their preferences. The few who referred to
agrarianism viewed the farmers' migration from farming
as an unwilling, imposed move. Hence, they described farmers
as victims of forces—government and agricultural programs
were the most cited protagonists—over which farmers
had no control but which nonetheless controlled their destinies.

TABLE 9. AGRARIAN EXPRESSION BY RESPONDENTS WHO HAD DESIGNATED MOVEMENT AS UNDESIRABLE: PERCENTAGE DISTRIBUTIONS OF RESPONSES FROM SOUTHEASTERN (1961) AND WESTERN KANSAS (1962)

Agrarian Expression	Farm Residents				Nonfarm Residents			
	General		Outstanding		Householders		College students	
	South-eastern	West-ern	South-eastern	West-ern	South-eastern	West-ern	South-eastern	West-ern
No. of Respondents	(54)	(51)	(18)	(58)	(115)	(195)	(15)	(43)
AGRARIAN THEMES	26.1	24.1	38.5	29.3	29.9	12.3	33.3	13.9
Independence	4.0	5.1	0.0	7.1	1.8	1.7	8.3	1.4
Fundamentalism	7.8	3.8	7.7	8.1	19.3	5.3	16.7	6.9
Moral virtues	14.3	15.2	30.8	14.1	8.8	5.3	8.3	5.6
FARMERS AS VICTIMS	7.8	8.9	11.5	6.1	12.9	11.3	12.5	11.1
Nonagrarian	66.2	67.1	50.0	64.6	57.3	76.4	54.2	75.0
Themes expressed:								
Percent	100.1	100.1	100.0	100.0	100.1	100.0	100.0	100.0
Number	(77)	(79)	(26)	(99)	(171)	(301)	(24)	(72)

TABLE 10. AGRARIAN EXPRESSION BY RESPONDENTS WHO HAD DESIGNATED MOVEMENT AS DESIRABLE: PERCENTAGE DISTRIBUTIONS OF RESPONSES FROM SOUTHEASTERN (1961) AND WESTERN KANSAS (1962)

| Agrarian Expression | Farm Residents | | | | Nonfarm Residents | | | |
| | General | | Outstanding | | Householders | | College Students | |
	South-eastern	West-ern	South-eastern	West-ern	South-eastern	West-ern	South-eastern	West-ern
No. of Respondents	(10)	(10)	(20)	(24)	(29)	(32)	(20)	(53)
AGRARIAN THEMES	0.0	0.0	0.0	0.0	0.0	2.4	0.0	0.0
Independence	0.0	0.0	0.0	0.0	0.0	0.0	0.0	0.0
Fundamentalism	0.0	0.0	0.0	0.0	0.0	2.4	0.0	0.0
Moral virtues	0.0	0.0	0.0	0.0	0.0	0.0	0.0	0.0
FARMERS AS VICTIMS	0.0	0.0	0.0	3.6	13.5	0.5	5.4	1.3
Nonagrarian	100.0	100.0	100.0	96.4	86.5	88.1	94.6	98.8
Themes expressed: Percent	100.0	100.0	100.0	100.0	100.0	100.0	100.0	100.1
Number	(10)	(14)	(26)	(28)	(37)	(42)	(37)	(80)

Perhaps "necessary" would have been a more appropriate term than "desirable" in this context. Movement was necessitated because the intervention of government in the agricultural economy appeared to impose two alternatives: increasing the scale of farm operations to remain full-time occupied in farming, or engaging in nonfarm occupations on a part- or full-time basis.

The overwhelming bulk of expressions—approximately 95 out of 100—articulated by those who regarded the move as a desirable one were nonagrarian in content. Their views considered agriculture as a declining industry in that it afforded few employment opportunities, or as one in which the capital demands for entrance precluded its being considered a reasonable alternative. Urban employment was regarded as an optimistic alternative for much of the redundant farm population. Some of these respondents indicated that living conditions, aside from employment opportunities, were so much better in the city that movement from farms was justified.

If all samples are aggregated, it is apparent that movement of population away from farm areas was, in large, considered undesirable. In this context, the ideology of agrarianism had become relevant as a symbol system for retaining farmers on the farm. An over-arching pessimism seems to qualify as a rationale for this expression. If farmers remained on the farm, they would not compete with city people for scarce nonfarm employment opportunities. Further, farm-reared youth would benefit from having spent their formative years in the rural environs.[19] Moreover, migrating farmers may overburden urban welfare rolls or be poverty-stricken because of their poor preparation for an urban labor force. While these arguments were more likely to have been articulated by nonfarm respondents, all were somewhat disposed to these views.

---

[19]The "moral virtue" element of agrarianism was specified by the Kansas respondents to a regard for the farm as "a good place to raise children." Every sample articulated this view.

One question remains. Taking the data over-all, it is apparent that southeastern Kansans, in comparison with their counterparts in western Kansas, were more given to expressing agricultural fundamentalism.[20] The western outstanding farmers were an exception; they articulated fundamentalism more than did their counterparts. The remainder of the discussion of the Kansas data will focus on this circumstance.

It will be recalled that analyses of the historical materials yielded the conclusion that fundamentalism was more frequently expressed in Massachusetts than in Kansas. That southeastern Kansans should more frequently cite this theme supports the earlier conclusion. The region of lower agricultural returns, where farming was a less often used option for earning a living, yielded more respondents who designated farming as the fundamental industry.

If residents of areas that are characterized by widely different agricultures marshal arguments that similarly cite agriculture's fundamentalistic nature, then their substantive views of farming differ. That western outstanding farmers, who undoubtedly represented rational farmers par excellence among the samples surveyed, articulated fundamentalism as did the southeasterners, led to the following hypothesis: much of the agriculture of an area with a declining economy constitutes a refuge whereas much of it in a growing economy constitutes a venture.[21] Designating farming as a refuge categorizes the farm as a last resort from which a minimum subsistence can be garnered. The farm is a consumption enterprise that provides a livelihood. In this conceptualization it is not an

[20]Respondents of the southeastern samples, except for the already noted exception of outstanding farmers category, expressed fundamentalistic themes two or three times more often than did their western counterparts.

[21]Social scientists will recognize a kinship between refuge and venture and Pareto's terms of *rentier* and *speculator*. Our concepts, in contrast to Pareto's, refer to social orientations to the use of resources. "Refuge" and "venture" constitute different definitions of the agricultural situation.

"employment" opportunity that yields financial income. The refuge form of farm employment yields a livelihood.

In an area where employment alternatives are increasing, more of those disposed to farming will be attracted to farming because it offers them gratifications equal to or greater than existing nonfarm alternatives. In some instances the gratifications will be financial.[22] Employment in this situation yields an income on which a living may be based. In this kind of area, it is much more likely that the farm will be conceptualized as a production enterprise with connections

TABLE 11.   NUMERICAL CHANGE IN THE TOTAL MALE RURAL
FARM POPULATION AND IN TWO AGE COHORTS OF THE
MALE RURAL FARM POPULATION, 1940–1960

Census and Cohort	Kansas	Southeastern Kansas	Western Kansas
1960 (Total)	166,982	18,590	17,680
1940 (Total)	321,278	40,559	28,033
Percent 1960 is of 1940	52.0	45.8	63.1
1960 (25–34 years)	14,121	1,275	2,100
1940 (5–14 years)	58,409	6,869	5,785
Percent 1960 is of 1940	24.2	18.6	36.3
1960 (60–69 years)	16,735	2,345	1,138
1940 (40–49 years)	38,977	4,537	3,250
Percent 1960 is of 1940	42.9	51.7	35.0

[22]In the nineteen counties of western Kansas (five of the counties had too few farm families on which to base an estimate of farm family income) for which 1960 data on farm family income and family income for the total population were available, the median farm income exceeded the median income for the county in five cases. The closest the farm family median income approached the median income for the total county in the southeast was 90 percent.

to markets. This is what was meant when it was stated that
agriculture offers an opportunity: this is venture agriculture.

To test the hypothesis, data were collected from the last three
censuses for age cohorts of the male rural farm population
residing in the two regions. (See Table 11.)
Studying a younger and an older age cohort and the extent
to which members of the cohort remained in or departed from
their region's farm population allows comparisons to be made
between the varieties of agriculture represented in these
areas of Kansas.

The younger cohort was made up of school-age males residing
in farm areas in 1940. By observing this cohort at two
later points in time, the midpoint of the group in 1950 being
an age—20 years old—when many men have made a
vocational commitment and the midpoint in 1960—30 years
old—being an age when men are even more firmly committed
to a vocation, we can compare the retention power of the
two agricultures. The older cohort was comprised of rural
farm males 40 to 49 years of age in 1940. By 1960, many
of this group would have reached the normal retirement age
of 65 years. The retirement age constitutes the cohort's
midpoint at the time of the latest census. The degree to
which an area retained or exported farm males was measured
by comparison to the Kansas rural farm male population
during the 20-year period.
An area with a declining economy would provide fewer
attractive employment opportunities to residents who were
youthful entrants to the labor force. It would be likely for
them to regard local enterprises as not affording employment
opportunities. On the other hand, older members of the labor
force in such an area would more likely continue, so long as
they were able, to fulfill occupational roles they had held
during their adulthood. This would be particularly so as a
chosen option for self-employed persons like farmers or
operators of retail establishments. With specific reference to
agriculture, it would seem to be the case that demand for
farm lands owned by older farmers would not be lively on the

part of persons seeking commercial farm units. It appears
to follow that the aged element in the rural farm population
would be disproportionately retained in an area with a
declining agriculture.

The data of Table 11 support the argument stated above.
The rural farm male population of the older cohort was
retained in southeastern Kansas by comparison to the state
figures. Proportionately fewer of this cohort was retained in
the west. Conversely, the younger cohort was more likely
to be retained in western Kansas than in the state or in the
southeast. Thus empirical evidence of the refuge or
venture qualities that have been applied to the varieties
of agriculture have been obtained.

Recourse to regional and national data allows an
opportunity to determine the generalizability of the Kansas
data: that is, do the analyses above constitute unique
occurrences that manifest social and economic circumstances
indigenous to Kansas farming?

Two samples of counties were drawn to answer the question.
One was regional and the other was a national sample.
The regional sample, comprised of the north central states,
was drawn to represent counties at the extremes of
farm-operator level-of-living indexes.[23] The classes

---

[23]Allan Beegle, Douglas Marshall, and Rodger Rice, "County
Migration Patterns in the North Central States, 1940–1950 and
1950–1960," NCR Res. Pub. No. 147 (Michigan Agricultural
Experiment Station, 1963). This publication classified each county
according to direction of migration, extent of manufacturing
employment, and farm operator level of living. The appendix table
listed each county by reference to the patterns that could be
derived from the logical combinations of the three factors. The
counties chosen from this sample were high or low for level of
living in both censuses and by reference to state and regional
means. The low-level-of-living counties were: Franklin, Massac,
Wayne of Illinois; Orange of Indiana; Chautauqua, Norton of
Kansas; Chippewa, Keweenaw, Schoolcraft of Michigan; Hubbard,
Mille Lacs of Minnesota; Barry, Dade, Madison, Polk, Taney of
Missouri; Pawnee of Nebraska; McKenzie of North Dakota; Guernsey,
Vinton of Ohio; Gregory of South Dakota; Ashland, Iron, Rusk
of Wisconsin (N = 24). The high-level-of-living counties were:
DeWitt, Livingston, Piatt of Illinois; Decatur of Indiana; Audubon,

of counties drawn to represent the region were similar
with reference to direction of migration and to the local
development of manufacturing. In the cited publication a
map (page 19) that portrays migration patterns indicates that
the low-level-of-living counties are concentrated in the
Ozark-Appalachian Highlands and the Lake States Cut-over
area, the remainder being distributed where rugged topography
or soil or moisture conditions restrict agriculture.
High-level-of-living counties, on the other hand, were most
likely to be found in the corn or wheat belts, the dairy areas,
or in those counties near metropolitan centers. A rough
correspondence between the two classes of counties drawn
from the region with the two areas of Kansas may be noted.
Similarly to the north central samples, the national sample
was chosen from a statistical report in which counties
were arrayed by farm-operator level-of-living indexes.[24]
Concentration of the low quintile counties in the

Clay, Hamilton, Kossuth, Palo Alto, Washington of Iowa; Clay,
Hodgeman, Ness of Kansas; Brown, Jackson, Murray, Stevens of
Minnesota; Atchison, Worth of Missouri; Dawson, Sheridan of
Nebraska; Renville of North Dakota; Logan of Ohio; Hyde,
Turner of South Dakota; Kewanee of Wisconsin (N=26).
One other note must be made: The inclusion of Kentucky in the
north central region is an administrative arrangement that makes
this region a different aggregation than is popularly thought of as
midwest. This addition, however, did not affect the samples drawn
because the counties selected were above or below the mean of
the region and the state as well.
[24]James D. Cowhig, "Farm Operator Level-of-Living Indexes, 1950
and 1960," Stat. Bull. No. 321, ERS (U.S. Department of
Agriculture, 1962). Table 2 of this publication was the source of
the list of counties from which a random sample was drawn of
those included in the lowest and highest quintiles. The level-of-
living index includes five items: average value of sales per farm,
average value of land and buildings per farm, percentage of farms
with telephones, home freezers, and automobiles. The Cowhig
publication utilized different items than had the earlier indexes.
The low quintile counties were: Escambia, Russell of Alabama;
Desha, Montgomery of Arkansas; Calhoun of Florida; Dawson,
Pickens, Polk of Georgia; Cumberland, Owsley of Kentucky;
Madison of Louisiana; Claiborne, Lawrence, Smith of Mississippi;
Wayne of Missouri; Madison of North Carolina; McCurtain of
Oklahoma; Anderson, Lauderdale of Tennessee; Harrison, Marion
of Texas; Greensville of Virginia; Wayne of West Virginia (N=23).
The high quintile counties were: Santa Clara of California; Broward,

southern United States is obvious, whereas the midwest accounts for two-thirds of the high quintile counties. Those counties of the nation that had level-of-living indexes of 29 or lower and those of 83 or higher in 1950 constituted the universes from which cases were randomly drawn.

TABLE 12.   NUMERICAL CHANGE IN THE TOTAL MALE RURAL FARM POPULATION AND IN TWO AGE COHORTS, 1940–1960, UNITED STATES AND TWO SAMPLES OF COUNTIES

Census and Cohort	United States	National Sample		North Central Sample	
		Lowest Quintile of FOLLI*	Highest Quintile of FOLLI	Lowest FOLLI	Highest FOLLI
1960 Total	6,956,657	43,781	69,723	40,408	74,046
1940 Total	12,078,610	145,820	125,099	92,726	109,911
Percent 1960 is of 1940	57.6	30.0	55.7	43.6	67.4
1960 (25–34 years)	582,131	3,146	6,036	2,959	7,231
1940 (5–14 years)	2,599,237	36,093	21,662	18,052	20,298
Percent 1960 is of 1940	22.4	8.7	27.9	16.4	35.6
1960 (60–69 years)	613,528	3,922	6,412	4,233	5,782
1940 (40–49 years)	1,404,080	13,151	15,533	10,236	13,511
Percent 1960 is of 1940	43.7	29.8	41.3	41.4	42.8

Palm Beach of Florida; Fulton, Morgan of Illinois; Clinton, Tippecanoe of Indiana; Cherokee, Iowa, Pocahontas of Iowa; Clay, Pratt of Kansas; Washtenaw of Michigan; Redwood of Minnesota; Cuming, Sheridan of Nebraska; Dutchess, Putnam of New York; Ashland, Sandusky of Ohio; Refugio, San Patricio of Texas; Chelan of Washington; Rock of Wisconsin (N=24).

*The term "FOLLI" employed in column headings refers to "Farm Operator Level of Living Index."

The analysis of age cohorts of the rural farm male
population between 1940 and 1960 compares with the Kansas
data in that greater declines of total population and of
the younger cohort are observed in the low-level-of-living
samples. (See Table 12.) However, both of these samples
depart from the Kansas analyses by reference to the retention
power of low income or level-of-living areas for older
males of the rural farm population. At any rate, refuge
agriculture constitutes a "push" situation as far as younger
males are concerned. The absence of alternatives for
entrants to the farm labor force is apparent in these
low-level-of-living farming areas.

The lack of confirmation for the observed outcome of
the Kansas analyses—the positive association between refuge
agriculture and retention of older rural farm males—suggested
an additional analysis. The *Census of Agriculture* provides
information on the number of farm operators of 65 years of age
or older and on the number of part-retirement farms in a
county.[25] It was hypothesized that refuge counties would be
the locales of higher incidence of part-retirement enterprises
than would the venture counties. Part-retirement farms are
distinguished from the more general category of part-time
farms by age of farm operator. For example, any farm whose
operator worked off the farm more than 100 days in 1959
and whose value of farm products sold was less than $2,500 was
a part-time enterprise. Part-retirement farms were those whose
operator's age was 65 years or older. Hence, in gross terms,
the incidence of greater fractions of part-retirees would
manifest retention in farming and smaller fractions would
manifest departures from agriculture.

The tabulations in Table 13 indicate that in both
samples a much greater number of older men in the refuge

---

[25]U.S. Bureau of the Census, *U.S. Census of Agriculture: 1959*, Vol.
I, Counties, Part for each State of which a county was a jurisdiction
(Washington: U.S. Government Printing Office, 1961). The source
used in each report was "County Table 5."

TABLE 13.   INCIDENCE OF PART-RETIREMENT FARMING AMONG
FARM OPERATORS AGED 65 OR OLDER, UNITED STATES
AND TWO SAMPLES OF COUNTIES, 1960 (ESTIMATES*)

		National Sample		North Central Sample	
	United States	Lowest Quintile of FOLLI	Highest Quintile of FOLLI	Lowest FOLLI	Highest FOLLI
Number of farm operators 65 years or older	617,270	4,663	5,212	4,636	3,997
Number of part-retirement farms	404,110	4,121	2,141	3,396	1,751
Percent part-retirement of total	65.5	88.4	41.1	73.3	43.8

*Because the "part-retirement" farm category is based on sampled
enumeration, these data are treated as estimates. Comparable percentages
for southeastern and western Kansas are as follows: southeastern Kansas,
2,507 operators 65 years of age or older of which 1,606, 64.1%, were
residing on part-retirement farms; western Kansas, 1,282 operators
65 years of age or older of which 213, 16.6%, resided on
part-retirement farms.

counties were farming than was the case in the venture
counties. The refuge counties exceeded the national incidence
by comfortable margins, whereas the venture counties
were well below the national figure. The Kansas data, which
are reported in the form of a footnote to Table 13, heighten
the distinctions that are observed in the regional or national
samples. To assess more fully the socioeconomic relevance of
the two agricultures lies beyond the province of the present
work. That additional work would be fruitful is clear.

Contemporary views of agriculture include the applications
of standards for assessing farming that amount to different
definitions of the situation. Government, which had been
importuned to assist farmers, has now become a scapegoat for
the ills of farmers. Sentiments consistent with agrarian
expression continue to be voiced by respondents who have

near or distant connections with farming. There appears to
be a reluctance to discredit wholeheartedly the morally
virtuous nature of farming. The taking of the view
that the "farm is a good place to raise children" overlooks
the mounting evidence that rural natives are relatively deprived
when they enter the contemporary labor force. Pure fresh
air, open space, and a school teacher who has training a few
short years beyond that of the pupils do not qualify as
substitutes for the laboratory equipment, library books, and
enriched curriculums to which the urban cousin has
been exposed.

We suggest that designating farming as a refuge or a venture
employs less ambiguous labels than do the labels of traditional
or rational, commercial or noncommercial, or the popular
phrases which specify farming as a way of life or farming
as a business. Refuge or venture agriculture constitute labels
that relate farming to other vocations and opportunities; these
terms also provide handles by means of which the infrastructure
of agriculture may be differentiated in connecting with
farmers and farm problems. The political and social relevance
of the refuge-venture dichotomy are considered in
the following chapter.

6
CONCLUSIONS
AND
INTERPRETATION

A large-scale society with an industrialized economy is
characterized by diverse, often discordant, sectors. Its census
of ideological expression is likely to be varied. By virtue of
the society's diversity, special-interest organizations will
promote viewpoints that counter those representing other
organizations. The contemporary civil rights controversy
constitutes a case in point. Each adversary has constructed
ideological expressions that provide suitable symbolic
rationales for the organization's operation. Further, the
formation of organizations promoting equal rights for nonwhites
engendered the formation of opposing organizations.

American political life offers another illustration of the
connection between ideology and organization. For example,
the forming of specific campaign organizations, "Businessmen
for Roosevelt" or "Labor for Goldwater," not only manifests
cognizance of popularly ascribed affiliations between party

and ideology but also constitutes attempts to persuade voters to change their dispositions in a single election. An objective of these campaign organizations is to diminish an organization's ideological character, thus emphasizing pragmatism over theory.

Rather than attending to the death or decline of ideology, the research question that guided this work concerned the effectiveness or ineffectiveness of ideological expression. Using American agrarianism in this context, the questions directing this study were: Who articulates or uses the ideology? To what issues does an ideology attach? How and why does an ideology persist?

While agrarianism was articulated by intellectuals who held an abiding faith in rural living, it has come to be used by people outside of agriculture. In fact, we have the impression that, in strength of numbers, its nonfarm advocates far exceed its advocates who remain on the land. The ideology has evolved from a rationale for agricultural issues to one that is applied in a variety of economic, political, and social situations. Indeed, its aesthetic applications may exceed its economic applications. The issues to which agrarianism has been attached and its nonfarm users show why it has persisted. It has motivational power and applicable scope beyond the limits of agriculture.

The evidence marshalled may be systematically concluded and interpreted by reference to the dichotomous or dualistic patterning that characterizes rural America. This pattern became apparent, as a generally applicable circumstance, in the course of this work. Those who participate in one of the agricultures are likely to use agrarianism differently from those in the other agriculture. For example, the venturing farmer will have a different rationale and use for a support price or conservation programs than will the farmer who seeks a refuge in agriculture.

A perception of the dualistic quality of American agriculture has led to a more inclusive understanding of rural circumstances. The two agricultures provide a framework for questions that structure the remainder of this chapter. What costs and benefits were realized by American farmers in the transition? What purposes do symbolic anchorages serve in the course of social change? What effects will present decisions have on the future of the rural population?

SOCIAL COSTS AND BENEFITS

The transition commenced in an economy that was almost wholly agricultural and in a context of prevailing localism in economic, political, and social arrangements. The urban-industrial advance diminished agriculture's economic and social dominance, but the rural population's political dominance was maintained long after its eminence in other sectors had been disconfirmed. In fact, the political institution afforded agriculture the means of mitigating the effects of the transition. The coincidental mixture of gains and losses that American farmers experienced undoubtedly obscured the objective conditions of agriculture in the transition.

As agriculture's portion of the national economy diminished, differential costs and benefits accrued to venturing or refuge-seeking farmers. The developing agricultural infrastructure—departments of agriculture, farm organizations, farmers' institutes, colleges of agriculture—was sought by commercial farmers or their advocates. The infrastructure largely constituted a direct benefit to farmers who sought an opportunity in agriculture. Consequently the same infrastructure was largely irrelevant to those who sought a refuge in farming. Moreover, it appears as though this irrelevance of the infrastructure to the refuge farmer has persisted to the present.

That government and political institutions emphasized local control and self-determination during the transition perhaps constituted a benefit to those who sought a refuge in agriculture. Undoubtedly some refugists obtained enough gratification from their independence of action to outweigh costs incurred by their (or their children's) nonparticipation in the developing economy. However, the chief costs of refuge agriculture may have been societal costs; the deprived environment produced poorly prepared entrants to the industrialized labor force, or the rural population, through its elected officials at the local, state or federal level, acted to stifle, restrain, or divert programs consistent with modernization.

The following illustrations indicate dimensions of costs and benefits as they were manifest in some situations. At the local level, more importance was attached to controlling education by employing teachers who would not contest reigning ideas than to employing teachers who would educate rural students for life in the industrialized city. In the context of agrarianism, this penchant manifested the social strength of the independent community populated by freeholding farmers. Apparently, the educational situation emphasized indoctrination of the young rather than development of their capacities to learn. It appears that teachers and clergymen, the two most numerous rural professionals who represented the "outside," were carefully scrutinized or quickly exported in order to restrict the expression of alien ideas and, perhaps, to prevent intergenerational conflict. The readily accepted outsiders were those who evinced cognizance of and appreciation for rural traditions. Moreover, they were expected to act to preserve traditional arrangements.

The aggressive support given to tradition must have inhibited those residents who would have been open to alien ideas. It is likely that many rural natives or outsiders residing in a community who were oriented toward innovation migrated because their views were not warmly received. This process of elimination had two results: many of those who felt stifled or oppressed by local traditions would migrate rather than contest long-standing customs; many of those who remained constituted a population to whom the traditional forms were attractive and who therefore socially supported traditional customs with unanimity. Perhaps this largely accounts for the widely acknowledged rural conservatism.

The industrial city was ambivalently regarded. Earlier we noted that it attracted and repelled simultaneously. When demands originating from urban populations required adaptation by farm or rural people, the demands were resented or rejected. The current stance taken by rural people and their legislators regarding legislative reapportionment is but the latest confirming incident in a consistent record. Curiously, however, the capricious market, the urban-inspired mechanism that could and did threaten farmers' financial circumstances, was not sufficient to destroy farming. For example, the low-income general farmer could feed his family and could obtain consumer goods by bartering his farm produce. Belt-tightening has been a time-honored rural response. Only in recent years has this response been regarded as a socially pathological situation. The man-made constraints on farming were painful but not fatal.[1] That farmers were able to translate their ability to survive discomfort into a virtue of rural living was noted earlier. It appears as though this ability was more characteristic of refuge agriculture. To the followers of this pattern, agriculture constituted a virtuous option to the rapacious city.

At this time we modify the view that the city was an attraction. It attracted some rural natives who became restless in the confines of the traditional rural universe. The attractive city drained these away. Those who remained in farming or village shopkeeping or those professionals who ministered to the needs of the resident population were more likely to have been repelled by the city. However, the city was by its presence relevant to them. Thus it constituted a problem to them to which at least grudging adaptation was made.

The emerging cities were objectively disagreeable residence places. The slums, sweatshops, and strife had been publicly

---

[1]We noted earlier that "unemployment" is a concept that has tended to be applied exclusively to describe urban economic conditions. Curiously, it appears that "underemployment" is a concept that was initially applied to rural circumstances. That these concepts had residential connections suggests that urban and rural economies differed in substance, form, and/or the points of view taken by observers.

recorded. It was reasonable to be repelled by the city. The nature of urban circumstances generated a social context such that the comparative attractions of rural America were articulated as social benefits. The origin for this articulation within agrarianism was that farming was the natural life. Cities were, within the context of this definition, unnatural. Even the urban dweller who enjoyed urban living would occasionally or frequently envy the farmer who could set his work schedule, live in pure surroundings, choose his representatives from an uncomplicated ballot, and know well his neighbors and political officials. Describing the city as unnatural was simultaneously a succinct expression of rural virtues and urban vices. Refuge agriculture epitomized an idyllic condition.

The farmers who sought a venturesome opportunity in agriculture differed markedly from the refugists in that they annually bore risks that yielded financial profits or losses. Their risks were compounded of the interaction of man-made and natural circumstances. Jaundiced observers of contemporary agriculture have had the venturing farmer in mind as they have noted that the farmer has the best of two worlds. These observers have mistakenly considered farmers as a homogeneous class. Our analyses and the literature we have surveyed indicate that farming includes diverse populations. In addition, the oversimplified view of agriculture obscures rather than advances understanding of rural America. For example, one way to regard the agricultural infrastructure is to assign it the purpose of reducing risks of those engaged in commercial production. Research directed toward increasing or improving farm production, legislative or executive actions oriented toward the amelioration of commercial agriculture, and educational efforts concerned with increasing the abilities of farmers are means of reducing risks. It is in this context that the agricultural infrastructure became affiliated with the interests of commercial or venturing farmers.

Whereas the refuge version of agriculture is most readily understood at the local level, it is more efficacious to view the venture version of agriculture from the vantage point of the state or federal levels within the governmental framework. The commercial farmer of the nineteenth century sought government intervention in his behalf. The legislation obtained by farmers in the half century between the Civil War and World War I manifested compliance with several actions sought by farmers. Executive programs of government were founded on the base of legislation. As executive agencies acquired specialized personnel and these professionals became tenured, they acquired vested interests in particular phases of agriculture. These agencies then became sites for the recommendation of policies and proposals relevant to farming. Undoubtedly, this was an unintended consequence to some of the participants in the farm protest movement. The unforeseen and unwanted development that nonfarmers became interested in setting policies for farming ramified widely in the agricultural industry. The mixed reaction to the Country Life movement was probably founded in this sort of circumstance.

Public policy development has received an imprint from this circumstance, also. A reason for the immobilization of farm policy during the past generation has been that remedial solutions for the farm problem have been offered both by farm organizations and by government agencies as well. The multi-centered infrastructure includes competing and conflicting segments. Thus far no one organization or combination has had sufficient power or authority to implement successfully its program as the means of resolution.[2]

The multi-centered constitution of the infrastructure involves two gross groupings. On the one hand, federal bureaus that are concerned with agricultural production problems, the commodity organizations, producers and marketing cooperatives, the American Farm Bureau, the bulk of the farm credit grantors, and a majority of the professional workers of the land-grant universities constitute an aggregation of agencies and groups

---

[2]However, there is some impressionistic evidence that one portion of the infrastructure has had sufficient authority to keep commercial farming as the central concern of the infrastructure.

that regard the problems of commercial agriculture as the farm problem. On the other hand, some social scientists of the land-grant system and of the federal government, the National Farmers Union, some of the consumers cooperatives serving farmers, and probably a majority of the rural life officials of the religious denominations constitute the aggregation of agencies and groups who attend to the problems of the refugists. The latter aggregation gradually assumed more influence between World Wars. Between the onset of World War II and the middle of the 1950's, this grouping had a declining influence. Apparently this aggregate has gained some influence in the last decade. The establishment of a series of programs to deal with rural poverty, the termination of the use of foreign laborers as contract harvest hands (an action that was obtained outside the constituted agricultural infrastructure) may be indicative of the rural American future. If this aggregation's power grows, it will be more popular to articulate the social dimensions of the farm problem than to focus narrowly upon the production problem.

However, we must note that those who attend to the problems of refugists are not so well informed in their approach to the farm problem; after all, measures dealing with production problems have a tangible character that makes them more visible and thus more readily subject to treatment. For example, the quinquennial *Census of Agriculture,* with its detailed treatment of crops and livestock statistics in conjunction with its less detailed treatment of social statistics, illustrates the disparity of factual information. Moreover, we have the impression that the collection of groups who focus on commercial agriculture are more in agreement as to means and ends than are those who are concerned with the noncommercial farm population.

The multi-centered nature of the infrastructure indicates that numerous groups or occupations, in addition to the farm population, hold investments in farming. It might be said, in this context, that the agricultural industry is as socialized, in cost-benefit terms, as any broad industry in the American economy. So it is that costs and benefits to be realized from agriculture's performance are widely diffused. Moreover, we can account, by reference to the rich extant literature, for the competitive and conflictive nature of many of the engagements within the infrastructure: a situation or occurrence that costs one segment, benefits another segment. Overproduction of feed grains costs feed-grain producers but benefits livestock men who purchase feed. Soybeans for margarine distresses dairymen while creating a new market for soybeans. Farm depression serves to increase employment in government agencies that have the objective of ameliorating economic and social problems of farmers. Not only is the investment in agriculture widely socialized but the antithetical outcomes that attach to specific occurrences will militate against the development of total consensus within the infrastructure. The decade ahead will be one of dissensus within the industry.

Undoubtedly a modern economy that involves a modernized agriculture will be characterized by an infrastructure. One characteristic of the infrastructure that has relevance for costs and benefits is its visibility. Policies and programs are largely hewn in public view. Costs and benefits tend also to be rendered visible. This provides us with the last item by means of which we will distinguish between the two agricultures. To a great extent, refuge-seeking farmers experienced gains or losses privately. Nostalgic literature may have glorified this pattern, and hence rendered the pattern social or public, but the empirical situations were and are individually experienced. It might be said that refugists, whatever their occupations, follow individualistic privatized patterns of response. However, as soon as an elaborate infrastructure has been developed, idiosyncratic, unique, or anonymous occurrences within commercial agriculture became less frequent. If one farmer, one area, or one sector of agriculture benefited from following a particular practice, it was likely that this good fortune was communicated to others. The American agricultural industry is characterized by an effective system of communication. Within agriculture there are no secrets. It has not been lack of information that accounts for the low productivity of refuge-seeking farmers. It is rather more likely that self-conscious choices they have made, or the inability to make a choice, account for the pattern they have followed. Choices engender real difficulties and risks of expanding operations and competing with established operators. No action is one response to such disagreeable alternatives.

Commercial farmers who have self-consciously sought information on innovations in agriculture and who have allied themselves with the infrastructure are not to be regarded as sinister persons who have subverted public institutions for self-aggrandizement. A mutually beneficial bargain has been struck among commercial farmers, county agents, farm organization officials, administrators and professionals of the land-grant universities, and the officials of the commodity organizations. The bargain has yielded a socially beneficial, efficient agriculture. The excluded segment of rural America requires a similar collection of organizations and agencies in order to relate meaningfully to the modernized economy that has evolved. The last section of this chapter considers this subject in more detail.

SYMBOLIC ANCHORAGES IN SOCIAL CHANGE

The occurrence of social change is objective. For example, recorded vital statistics factually indicate the contours of social change. The way representatives of labor and management negotiate now as compared with the nature of their interaction one generation in the past manifests social change. Changes. over time in the requirements of a job, in organizational styles, in the conduct of a nation's foreign policy, are illuminated by comparing the present with past arrangements. Empirical evidence of change is abundant and, in many cases, unequivocal.

That agriculture had changed was not problematic for this study. However, American agriculture provided an opportunity to observe a changing industry that appeared to connect with an essentially unchanging ideological expression. It had been demonstrated that ideology persists despite disconfirmation; its persistence appeared to be related to its being of symbolic importance to a group or to some aggregate of a population. Social support for an ideology, a collection of interacting adherents who are similarly disposed, allows it to withstand erosion.

Our analyses suggest that agrarian expression has four bases in the context of refuge agriculture. The articulation of a specific base manifests an anchorage utilized as change is under way or imminent. No claim is made that the full spectrum of anchorages has been explicated in this work.

In an eastern area where urban-industrial opportunities were nearby and in which the city offered preferable alternatives to agricultural employment, numerous expressions of agrarianism were voiced. Printed remarks of the Massachusetts reports praised or damned farmers. Their laudatory features noted that migration from eastern farm areas had built the cities and the successful western farms; farm production sustained the cities; farms and cities were mutually necessary. Although some urban institutions made unseemly demands of farmers, it was advisable to adapt to the demands. Moreover, certain farmers, the unadaptable, constituted a socially pathological category. They were exhorted to exorcise themselves of their delinquencies and to match strides with contemporary developments.

Hence, refuge agriculture proximate to urban-industrial development received two interpretations. On the one hand, the refuge was a magnificent fund of talent that served, without peer, to provision the American economy, polity, and society. This usage of refuge implied that eastern agriculture had been a reservoir from which other sectors or regions obtained their cadres of enterprisers. While some evidence buttressed this view, the provincial stance required discounting or ignoring contributions from numerous elements of the American population. That the reservoir had so mightily contributed to national development was an ethnocentristic expression of the fundamental nature and virtuous character of eastern agriculture. Further, this version of the refuge was a glorification of the past. Dividends were being or had been collected on Americans' investment in eastern agriculture.

The second interpretation by the Massachusetts reports of refuge agriculture near the developing city was that agriculture served as a shelter for those who would not or could not match the times. In a general sense, the refuge was a sanctuary for ne'er-do-wells. Refugists manifested lethargy or passivity to the demands being made by an industrializing economy; their lethargy was especially manifest in their adherence to customs of another era; they were unenlightened and chances were good that their ignorant dispositions would be socially transmitted to their heirs; they lacked a discernible interest in self-improvement. Perhaps the more recently identified void between professional agricultural workers and low-income farmers was initially developed in this context.

Representatives of this interpretation of refuge agriculture (it must be noted that the pattern was designated by agents of change) disconfirmed two elements of the agrarian ideology: refugists failed to fulfill the expectations of the morally virtuous engaged in a fundamental industry. That they exemplified the independent yeoman was discredited or disregarded. Perhaps fiction writers were the principal articulators of the positive values of this variety of agriculture. Participants in the negative version of the refuge were contemporaries of the advocates of change. It appeared as though these refugists were a blot on eastern agriculture's record.

Two bases for refuge agriculture, one suggested by the historical evidence and one by present-day findings, may be discerned from the Kansas data. The current evidence will be treated first.

Data collected from southeastern Kansas residents suggest that belt-tightening persits as a viable response among rural Americans. Whether farmers who go it alone, stoically meeting the circumstances that confront them, are refugists or trapped is a moot question. Farming with a limited resource base appears to be an option chosen when nonfarm alternatives are not preferred, or are unknown, unattractive, or declining.[3] Perhaps the participants obtain sufficient rewards from fulfilling self-definitions concerning independent behavior and morally

---

[3]Frederick C. Fliegel, "Aspirations of Low Income Farmers and Their Performance and Potential for Change," *Rural Sociology,* 24, No. 3 (1959), 205–14. Fliegel's incisive analysis supports the general argument we pose.

virtuous conduct. In an earlier study, one of the authors noted that farmers who did not participate in extension educational programs manifested an unusually high degree of self-confidence in their farming abilities.[4]

The social fissure between agents of change and low-income farmers, a fissure that is indicated by a communication gap and lack of rapport, may have resulted from reciprocal rejection. The void will be doubly difficult to bridge if this view is accurate. It seems reasonable to conclude, therefore, that quite different answers to a straightforward question such as "What is farming?" would be given by refugists and professional agricultural workers.

A theme extracted from the Kansas reports indicated that the promised land had been ravaged. Farmers were hampered from gaining a satisfactory living by natural and man-made circumstances. Moreover, ironically, rural natives migrated to urban residence. The first task was to recreate rural communities whose residents had been innocent victims. When schoolhouses and churches were once again in full use, renovation would be realized. Recruiting teachers and clergymen sympathetic with rural life would be an initial step. Following these steps, if all would work toward renovation, the full promise of rural life would be obtained.

We have framed a hypothesis that accounts for this posture: The last land frontier had been translated into the final American agricultural opportunity. While eastern farmers had had a farm alternative in western land resources, those who farmed in the West had no such option. The exhaustion of the store of pre-emptable land clouded the present and the future. This hypothesis suggests that expressers of this theme overstressed the national relevance of the farm population as they understressed the gains to be made from increasing agricultural productivity.

The landed domain provided more than bread alone in their view. If rural living conditions were allowed to deteriorate, the

---

[4]Wayne C. Rohrer, "On Clienteles of the Agricultural Extension Service," *Rural Sociology*, 20, Nos. 3–4 (1955), 302–03.

people who lived in or migrated from these areas would
undermine the American promise. The view involved a
restatement of agriculture as the fundamental industry.

The closing of the frontier was undoubtedly one impetus in the
calling of the Country Life Commission. On hindsight, the
Commission and reactions to its proposals were of such a nature
as to constitute a watershed event. Persons affiliated with this
movement noted that America without a strong farm population
was a weakened America or a markedly different nation from
the one wanted by many citizens. The report suggested means
of ameliorating rural living conditions. Government intervention
undergirded by welfare motives would reduce rural deprivation.
Farm residents and private and public agencies were to rebuild
rural communities through organization. The refuge had been
articulated as a sanctuary that would repay national interest
were it restored and conserved. The accomplishment of
restoration and conservation required public and private efforts.
The evolving infrastructure was to be concerned with farm
production problems and social problems as well.

However, observers who alleged that the Commission represented
the interests of sentimental do-good nonfarmers noted that the
ills of agriculture would be alleviated by increasing productivity.
Land was only one factor of production. Migration from farms
was not to be decried per se; some migration was efficacious.
For example, contemporary data collected from outstanding
farmers of southeastern Kansas would suggest that some
venturing farmers regard out-migration of farmers as an
opportunity for those who remain to obtain more efficient
enterprises.

The watershed nature of this episode may be concluded as
follows: The farm community had differentiated into a rural
community in which some were productively engaged in farming
and others were not so engaged. The latter were refugists.
Recommendations that would have aided the refugists were not
implemented; nor have the problems of low-income farmers
ever been an extensive or central concern to the infrastructure
as constituted. More recent public programs constructed to deal

with rural poverty give promise of success to the extent that these programs will be or are established outside the confines of the infrastructure. Even as early as World War I, productively engaged farmers could be designated as venturing farmers. They incorporated the agricultural infrastructure into their farm management plans.

The conjuncture of the behavior of venturing farmers and governmental actions in behalf of agriculture yielded the excluded segment of rural communities. Blunting the objectives of public programs concerned with social problems has caused policy-makers to be perennially confronted with rural poverty. Busy engagement with other issues has allowed some policy-makers to ignore this development. Others have ingenuously or cynically used agrarianism as a rationale for not taking remedial action. A few policy-makers have addressed themselves to the perennial issue. The control exercised by legislators oriented toward agrarianism, or whose gerrymandered constituencies are overly representative of farming interests, has determined the direction of executive programs. Agency administrators who have been aware of rural social problems have been constrained from acting on nonproduction problems.

Primary and secondary data have specified the social characteristics of venturing farmers. It is fruitful to consider some outcomes of this venturing pattern that have not previously been treated.

A venture agriculture will be accompanied by the development of many occupational specialties that supplement farm entrepreneurs: dealers in feed, seed, fertilizer, insecticides, weed killers, irrigation or drainage equipment, farm implements; personnel of private or public agencies providing services of credit, agricultural education, employee recruitment, management assistance; field men of cooperatives, farm organizations, management services, processing or marketing organizations, and vertically integrated enterprises; labor contractors; wage laborers; veterinarians; and health inspectors. The venturing farmer will relate directly to a legion of specialized talents holding an interest in his enterprise.

The conduct of the venture farm enterprise includes decision-making by some who have specialized competence; the accuracy of the farmer's judgment in assessing the technical capacities of specialized experts possibly has more relevance for the success of his enterprise than any other decision he makes. As he purchases services and decision-making capacities, he reduces technical risks but increases the scale of involvement in the enterprise. The farmer is an executive. This is what was meant when we stated that modern agriculture is a highly socialized industry. Future circumstances of venture agriculture will most likely involve a further differentiation of the occupations that impinge on the farm enterprise. Larger farm enterprises will undoubtedly match this differentiation with employed assistants who will coordinate several specialties that apply to the enterprise.

One version of refuge agriculture was an articulation by nonfarmers who glorified the past. Their remarks, which denied the present and future, essentially wrote off agriculture as a viable alternative for their area. Some nonfarm contemporaries of refugists derogated this mode of farming. Their ethnocentristic moralizing was long on hortatory advice but short on compassionate understanding. Other nonfarm contemporaries decried the social circumstances of rural living in general. Their militant activism was honored verbally but has never received the support of power wielders. Some contemporaries view the refuge as a respected employment chosen by farmers who have no occupational alternatives. This laissez-faire view acknowledges the presence of refugists.

The transition to industrialization constituted a societal economic change that impacted domestic agriculture. In one way or another, refuge agriculture failed to keep step with the economic development. After breaking step with the national thrust, refugists were largely unaffected by the transition. Conversely, perhaps the refugists affected the transition to the extent that they constituted a human resource that was not readily useful to an industrialized economy in an urbanized society.

On the other hand, venturing farmers matched strides with the transition. Their conduct took account of present circumstances but allowed them a measure of effect on future arrangements as well. Involvement with the infrastructure of agriculture and representation by special-interest groups yielded them entree to extra-local institutions and organizations. One way they affected the future was through the overrepresentation of rural areas in legislative halls. Through these and other specified means they negotiated the transition and have been responsible for constructing an agriculture whose productive capacity is the envy of the world.

CONTEMPORARY DECISIONS AND THE FUTURE OF RURAL AMERICA

George Herbert Mead's observation that the present emerges out of the past and the future emerges out of the present is sharply etched in the time sequence that obtains in the specification of a problem, and the future consequences that result from having taken a particular policy line. Enacted legislation is a public expression of an attempt at problem solution. The Homestead Act, the Morrill Act, the Smith-Lever Act, and others related to farm concerns apparent at the time of passage. Legislation solves some problems. However, all legislation is anachronistic to a degree: it solves problems that were apparent prior to the time of passage. In some instances an imperfect fit between enactment and the subject of treatment will obtain. The poorest fit probably occurs in instances where rapid change is under way, or when representation is not representative. Also, enacted legislation has had unforeseen consequences. The 160-acre limitation of the size of Great Plains farms pre-empted under the Homestead Act is a case in point. One hundred and sixty acres was a farm in the eastern Middle West, but only a fraction of a farm in the western Middle West. The relevant points: past circumstances affect decisions and decisions have future consequences.

In a pathbreaking essay, Boulding noted that we will depart from the traditional methods that have been used in teaching and training as we acquire abilities "to learn from rapidly changing systems."[5] Hence, some contemporary issues will not be satisfactorily confronted if we adduce guidelines solely from past procedures or if our adaptations are restricted to those supported by testimony of special-interest pleaders. We submit that viable alternatives may be adduced from the literature provided by the fund of social research of the last generation.[6] Extant literature bearing on our research problem has yielded convincing evidence of the fruitfulness of the accumulated knowledge. Moreover, recourse to the fund has a practical rationale: whereas, in the past, years were available for collecting testimony and weighing alternatives preparatory to decision-making, we now have a more stringent time budget.

The ways that public agencies have connected with the farm population in the course to industrialization have been discussed. Government assistance was sought initially to control nonfarm threats to agriculture. Later policies featured indemnification, restitution, and financial subsidization of the farm population. The shifting context of policies involved a changing social universe in which decisions were taken. The evidence indicates that a flexible posture has been characteristic of public policies oriented toward commercial agriculture. It seems reasonable that the adaptability of the past with regard to one agricultural sector will be applied to the development of programs consistent with the needs of refuge farming. However, it appears as though the generous time span, the approximately three human generations required for the evolution of policies toward commercial farming, will not be available to policy-makers to act on problems of refuge agriculture.

Undoubtedly dynamic policies toward commercial agriculture were founded somewhat in the disproportionate

[5]Kenneth Boulding, "Where Are We Going If Anywhere? A Look at Post-Civilization," *Human Organization*, 21, No. 2 (1962), 162–67; quote from page 167.

[6]Robert S. Lynd, *Knowledge for What?* (Princeton: Princeton University Press, 1939). Not only does Lynd's work support our argument but it constitutes evidence par excellence of the fruitful literature that has been available for a generation or more.

rural representation in legislative bodies. Disproportionate
representation based on residence has been declared
unconstitutional. We suggest that the public response to rural
social problems will be enhanced if, in contrast to tradition,
we no longer regard residential aggregates as having unusual,
idiosyncratic qualities. For example, unemployment or underemployment have economic, political, and social relevance
whether they are urban or rural-based. Once again we hark back
for a policy suggestion to a view expressed one generation ago,
Goldschmidt's recommendation that farm laborers needed an
analogue to the Extension Service.[7] We would generalize his
recommendation to note that several populations included in the
agricultural industry require public attention. Were the
organizations created to implement these programs to be initiated
outside the present agricultural infrastructure, as we earlier
recommended, they would probably become incorporated in the
infrastructure with the passage of time. In this view, the
infrastructure will include more diverse organizations in the
years ahead.

The organizations and agencies affiliated with American
agriculture markedly increased in number during the course to
industrialization. Additional increments to this collection will be
consistent with the secular trend. Despite the competing or
conflicting orientations represented within the infrastructure, a
common interest in farming allows the inclusion of a diverse
collection in a single structure. By the same line of reasoning,
new organizations would be incorporated.

For the future, it appears as though the complex economy and
polity will be paralleled by a verdant growth of groups and
agencies. We speculate that as a new organization becomes part
of the infrastructure, specification of its means and ends will
serve to limit its purview. Some issues will be bared that lie
just outside the provinces of organizations in being. The
confronting of these issues will constitute a rationale for a new
orientation; the new orientation may be acted upon by existing

---

[7]Walter Goldschmidt, *As You Sow* (New York: Harcourt,
Brace and Co., 1947), Chapter X.

agencies that modify means and ends or by the initiation of new agencies. In a gross sense, it appears that initiation of a new organization is more likely than is modification of an existing organization. One sequence followed in the initiation of new groups may be gleaned from our limited analysis: An active minority directs the attention of legislators and/or public agency personnel to an issue; public servants express interest and concern and direct some, albeit limited, attention to the issue; a special-interest organization and a public agency form around an important persisting issue.

This account indicates that a joining of public and private efforts has been characteristic of the formulation of public policy in American agriculture. The proposed sequence has never been fully realized with regard to nonexpressive refuge agriculture. Perhaps the breakdown has occurred in that public agencies have restricted the expression of interest and concern to the publication of reports. Agencies have not been initiated to deal with the problems delineated by the reports. And a characteristic of those who are employed in refuge agriculture is that they are nonarticulate and are therefore easily ignored.

On the face of it the noninitiation of organizations to deal with refugists' problems is ironic. It is ironic because one clear expression of the American genius is represented in willingness to create new organizations to deal with issues that have been ignored, unacknowledged, or bypassed. The New Deal era of the federal government was characterized by the intiation of organizations. Apparently we have sufficient treasure to create wholly new organizations while we finance existing organizations. Perhaps this affluence constitutes an idiosyncratic characteristic that distinguishes this nation from the remainder of the world. However, the initiation of a new organization perhaps requires the formation of a special-interest group whose expressions are effective. The collection that has formed around refuge agriculture has not been able to obtain sustained and meaningful action.

The initiation of land-grant colleges at a time when hundreds of private schools were in operation illustrates this circumstance.

The contentions that private colleges failed to offer educational opportunities to the general public and that classical training did not meet the requirements of an industrializing economy were rationales for the new publicly supported colleges. Moreover, private and public universities have co-existed for decades. A hypothesis on the context in which we initiate organizations is suggested: An organization is generally initiated to supplement or complement existing organizations rather than to supplant them. One hundred years of hindsight confirms this in regard to land-grant and private universities.

A related conclusion, which requires further testing, involves the restatement of an economic proposition stated by George Foster, an anthropologist. He noted that under conditions of peasant agriculture the production pie is regarded by villagers as having a constant size.[8] Thus if an individual or family prospers, this prosperity is regarded as having been at the expense of the remainder of the community. The American ethos contradicts this. In the American experience the pie has grown larger. The views of economists support this notion. The pie represented by the number of groups and organizations has had an ever enlarging circumference. Perhaps America has no national peer in this context.

Willingness to create new organizations does not constitute the sole way in which social means are adapted to deal with human problems, however. It is not contended that an organization is rigidly confined to its original objective(s). Once again the land-grant institutions offer illustrative evidence of organizational growth. As these universities engaged in instructional activities the inadequate research base became apparent. The experiment stations were initiated to obtain such a base. Later, when it became apparent that practicing farmers were not utilizing the fund of information provided by research, the addition of an adult educational agency was proposed. The extension service was initiated to carry research results to farmers. Actions

---

[8]George M. Foster, *Traditional Cultures and The Impact of Technological Change* (New York: Harper and Brothers, 1962), pp. 52–53.

consistent with the original charter of the land-grant colleges had indicated social needs that were not considered at the initiation of the colleges.

Both the growth of an organization and its areas of interest are limited in fact. That the agricultural infrastructure has never given central attention to noncommercial farmers illustrates a limitation. The environment imposes some limits. The interests of employed personnel set limits. Sponsors or clients of an organization may also articulate bounds for an organization's action.

When available organizations do not fulfill credible social needs or when they will not modify their activities to encompass a newly discerned area of operation, a new organization is initiated. The articulation of unmet social demands constitutes an ideological expression that serves to energize those who seek change. Expression of a demand that receives social support (social support refers to number of adherents and to intensity of commitment) is translated into an organizational form. That this is a time-honored American response is supported by de Tocqueville's observation of more than one century ago of the American penchant to form organizations as the means of dealing with human problems.[9] The formation of an organization utilizes a social rationale, oftentimes in the form of an ideological expression, as a symbolic basis for its initiation. Moreover, the initiation of an organization manifests an interest in the seeking of change.

The initiation of organizations, analogously to the initiation of new occupations, does not constitute an unequivocal social gain. The American ethos is remarkably permissive in that Americans are encouraged to form associations.[10] Nevertheless,

---

[9]Alexis de Tocqueville, *Democracy in America*, edited by H. S. Commager and based on Henry Reeve's original translation (New York: Oxford University Press, 1947), pp. 319–20.

[10]Robin M. Williams, Jr., *American Society, A Sociological Interpretation*, 2nd ed. (New York: Alfred A. Knopf, 1960), pp. 494–501, for documentation of the proliferation of associations and the permissive atmosphere that is conducive to their initiation.

neither what we have written nor Williams' remarks should be construed as a prediction of an emerging Utopian social order. The initiation of new organizations will further fragment interpersonal relationships and make coordinative positions and organizations more crucial than at present. The coordinative organizations—councils of churches, civic councils, interstate compacts—that have developed to integrate certain activities of autonomous organizations will probably become more elaborate in the future. A major portion of the agricultural infrastructure was coordinated in this fashion during the decade of the 1920's. If additional organizations are initiated to deal with the issues of refuge agriculture and these organizations are incorporated into the infrastructure, there will be greater need for coordination.

Much of the discussion of decision-making has been devoted to considerations of refuge agriculture. We regard this issue as a paramount concern in America today. However, it is likely that the future holds change for those engaged in venture agriculture. The diminution of the farm population will affect venture farmers as some of them incorporate additional tracts of land into their farm enterprises. In this respect the future constitutes an extrapolation from the past. Undoubtedly, a larger fraction of the venturers will employ crews of laborers at certain times in the growing season. Venture farmers will allocate more time to decision-making and managing employees than heretofore. The decline in the farm population will not be directly paralleled by a decline in the number of venture farmers. Venturing enterprisers and employed wage workers will probably account for an increasing fraction of the farm population.

It appears plausible that the venture sector of agriculture will undergo organizational changes in the future. Additional applications of vertical integration seem certain. Horizontal integration, the linking together of several farms each of which produces the same farm product, is another means of enlarging the farm enterprise to use inputs more efficiently. The effect of this organizational form is largely unknown because of the lack of availability of published statistics. However, horizontal integration makes good economic sense and is probably a mode

of adaptation followed by venturing farmers. Apropos either kind
of integration: the future production of food products consumed
by Americans may be more substantially based in foreign
countries than is presently the case. Therefore it seems reasonable
to conclude that neither vertical nor horizontal integration will
be confined by U. S. national boundaries.

New organizational forms would not necessarily be confined
to innovations contained within the private economic sector. For
example, it is conceivable that the food production industry
would be defined as a public utility. Agriculture, like the
enterprises distributing water, electricity, and natural gas is
privately managed but is carried on somewhat under public
auspices as well. Agriculture of the venture sort is implicated in
private and public sectors. However, monopolistic control is
present only for a few farm commodities, whereas publicly
awarded franchises grant monopoly power to utilities firms.
Moreover, the number of farm enterprises, even restricting
the universe to those of venture agriculture, vastly outnumber
the utilities firms. On the other hand, some comparability
exists. Obviously, food is a necessity just as are the services
provided by public utilities. Both agriculture and the public
utilities involve private and public sources of decision-making.
While we do not propose that food production be designated a
public utility, to do so would resolve some agricultural issues.
For example, wages paid to hired workers, controlling the uses
of insecticides, price policies of farm products, and
conservation programs probably would be efficaciously
administered in this context.

Our hope is that this work will become a part of the social
science fund of knowledge and that the total fund will be used
by busy legislators, agency administrators, and social
researchers. In our view, the clarification of social circumstances
is fundamental to contemporary decision-making.

Some of the decisions that have been rendered visible in
American foreign policy efforts are considered in the following
chapter. We endeavor there to connect domestic concerns
with foreign adventures.

7

FOREIGN
ADVENTURES
OF
UNITED STATES
AGRICULTURE

The involvement of American agriculture with international
affairs was an inevitable result of its productive capabilities,
coupled with a continuing partnership between public and
private enterprises dedicated to improving production.
Rational agriculture, as described earlier, began in the
mid-twentieth century to exhibit unforeseen capacity to produce
for the market. Historical evidence does not as yet satisfactorily
uncover the reasons for this phenomenon; the conditions
of production and marketing, however, have become matters
of increasing urgency. The geometric increase in innovations
which substitute machines for men has continued with
general disregard for the phenomenon of underemployment
on the farms. The background of this development can be traced
from World War I. The efforts that had been made to improve
agricultural production by generous land policies, by
reclamation and conservation interests, and by establishment of
agricultural services suddenly found a new justification in high

prices and national loyalty expressed in the 1915 slogan, "Food will win the War." Multiple stimuli to produce brought positive results. Vast areas of virgin soil were brought under the plow and from 1915 to 1920 a feverish boom in agriculture ran its course. Production of wheat, for example, increased during these years by 50 percent while farm income as a whole nearly trebled.[1]

With restoration of European agriculture and the removal of other wartime abnormalities, U. S. agriculture, geared to supply food to Europe during the war period, entered a long period of imbalance between production and available market. Efforts to restore a balance involved both agriculture and government in foreign as well as domestic activities; it is the former with which we are principally concerned in this chapter. The relevant topics are (1) foreign trade in farm commodities, (2) missions to improve foreign agriculture, and (3) the foreign agricultural systems and their capacities for change.

FOREIGN TRADE IN FARM COMMODITIES AFTER WORLD WAR I

Domestic demand for farm products in the 1920's failed to keep up with production capabilities developed in wartime. Replacement of draft animals with tractors freed fifty million acres of grain and forage crops for food production. The modest population growth was more than offset by a notable tendency to consume less per capita of cereals, pork products, and starchy foods. Urban life, that of a majority of Americans after 1920, imposed dietary standards that altered the demands for farm products. Demands for textiles also underwent significant shifts, to the disadvantage of cotton and wool producers.

As prices for farm products tumbled after 1920, policy-makers groped for relief. The first resort was to protect against imports by means of higher tariff rates, and these rates were

---

[1]Merle Fainsod, Lincoln Gordon, and Joseph Palamountain, *Government and the American Economy* (New York: W. W. Norton and Co., 1959), p. 131.

raised three times during the decade. As it became obvious that increased tariff rates would not help the farm marketing situation, proposals were aimed at bolstering domestic prices against world market prices. The most widely publicized of these was the McNary-Haugen bill, first introduced in Congress in 1924 and finally passed in 1927 and again in 1928, only to be killed both times by presidential veto. These measures sought to make tariff legislation effective by taking off the domestic market through government purchase that portion of farm produce necessary to maintain prices at a level equivalent to those of the 1909–1914 period. Excess production was to be sold abroad at world prices. The deficit incurred in the transaction would be recovered by a tax on domestic sales. The two-price concept became an avidly proposed alternative during and after the McNary-Haugen debates.

On the domestic scene, a high degree of concern for the commercial farmer was shown by the passage in 1921 of the Packers and Stockyards Act, which provided for national inspection and regulation of stockyards and packers engaged in interstate commerce. Both rates charged and conditions of operation became subject to federal approval. Likewise, the Grain Futures Act of 1922, the Produce Agency Act of 1927, and the Perishable Agricultural Commodities Act of 1930 reflected efforts to protect the farmers from middlemen.

Another evidence of concern for the marketing function was the enactment in 1922 of the Capper-Volstead Act offering preferential treatment, including immunity from antitrust proceedings, for farm cooperatives. This policy was furthered in the Agricultural Marketing Act of 1929, which provided governmental credits in the formation of a gigantic cooperative marketing system and also established a Federal Farm Board with capital for purchasing and marketing grain so as to maintain prices at an acceptable level and build stockpiles for emergencies.

It may be noted that the policies of the period were designed to assist the farmer as a businessman in difficulties with marketing conditions. They were designed to rationalize the efforts of the agricultural sector, all of which was viewed as a part of the system of business and commerce. In regard to foreign trade, the basic premises were strongly nationalistic, even isolationist. Regardless of euphemisms employed to make the programs domestically acceptable, critics at home and in foreign lands pointed out that the intention was to dump surpluses on foreign markets. European nations reacted with tariff policies and programs that made our own look like child's play. Foreign trade dwindled and the problems of agricultural marketing grew.

Some relief from the restrictions of high tariff policy was obtained following the enactment of the Reciprocal Trade Agreements Act of 1934. The high tariff rates of the three years preceding had caused a precipitous drop in agricultural exports, from an annual value of 1.8 billion dollars to .8 billion dollars. By the end of 1934, ad valorem rates on farm products averaged 35 percent below the 1932 level. The trend toward freer trade in farm products made a contribution toward the internationalization of American agriculture and illuminated the dimensions of the problems of world agriculture.

Although foreign policy in agriculture has gone on into much more complex developments, some of the domestic concepts that were introduced during the period under discussion have continued and have become permanent parts of public policy. These include the two-price system discussed above, domestic allotments, and the concept of parity for farm products in the market. The elaborate farm programs commenced in the 1930's and continuing to the present have incorporated these basic features. The objectives of foreign policy underwent extensive evolution after World War II; this evolution contains in its own way the record of the dilemmas and tribulations of modern American agriculture.

WORLD WAR II AND ITS AFTERMATH

Up to the time of the invasion of Poland in 1939, U. S. agriculture had presented the picture of "plenty in the midst of depression." The problem of obtaining for commercial farmers a satisfactory market for their produce remained unsolved. The situation for farmers had been slightly alleviated, but at the cost of very complex and expensive programs and extensive governmental participation in the market. In 1940, for example, the Commodity Credit Corporation had under either loan or purchase one-third of the wheat raised, one-fourth of the cotton crop, and one-third of the flue-cured tobacco. The Corporation dealt heavily in other farm commodities.[2] The far-reaching activities of the Department of Agriculture had caused the budget for that department to reach a billion dollars by 1939. (By 1966 it had grown to seven billion.)

World War II temporarily alleviated the problems of surpluses and marketing. Farmers responded to eased restrictions on production and high prices. Food production was increased by 50 percent over that attained in World War I; it was accomplished on substantially the same acreage and with 10 percent less manpower and serious shortages of machinery and supplies.[3]

Under the pressure of war emergency, the congressional farm bloc operated with great efficiency to maximize economic gains. Guarantees that the commercial sector of agriculture would be protected and promoted were continued in even stronger terms.[4]

The policies, aided by powerful production technologies, again resulted in the accumulation of massive surpluses, for which the government now faced inescapable responsibilities. Commodity Credit Corporation inventories reached almost six billion dollars in 1957. The costs of storage added to the costs of operating the

---

[2]W. W. Wilcox, *The Farmer in the Second World War* (Ames: Iowa State College Press, 1947), p. 27.

[3]*Ibid.,* p. 24.

[4]The political struggle over details of the farm subsidy programs need not be examined here. Two characteristics of the struggle are of significance to the theses of this book: (1) the struggle resulted in a wider separation of the rational and the traditional farmers; in crude terms, "the rich grew richer . . ."; (2) the issues usually divided the commercial farmers into commodity and regional groups and alliances, with the traditional farmers constituting a kind of dissenting voice, not strong enough to exercise a balance of power position.

program began to react on the political climate, and there was mounting criticism of agricultural policies. The temporary solutions of World War II were gone; the continued "cold war," even the Korean conflict and several brush-fire outbreaks, by no means served the same purpose. Most of the old problems dating at least from 1920 were back again, some in an intensified form.

Not unnaturally, the possibilities of foreign marketing were continually probed by those interested in the welfare of agriculture. Means of disposing of farm products abroad bore the mark of true Yankee ingenuity, and between 1940 and 1960 over 20 billion dollars were spent by the government on foreign aid programs aimed at the disposal of farm commodities.[5]

Among the motivating forces back of the proliferation of foreign programs in agriculture the following appear to be most prominent: (1) the need for preserving the solvency of the commercial farmer, (2) the availability of surpluses which were costly to store, (3) the "discovery" of "backward" agriculture in foreign countries that could benefit from modernization (and apparently wanted these changes), (4) a contest with the Soviet Union for spheres of influence in underdeveloped lands, and (5) a strong belief in missionary enterprise and in an "American way of life" which placed a high value on its agrarian characteristics. The motives can be seen reflected in varying proportions in the major international farm programs developed since 1950. Not all of these can be discussed here, but major ones, illustrative of the many-pronged policies, are summarized below. It may be noted, and emphasized, that the foreign ventures of agriculture have been based on a desire to strengthen commercial agriculture at home. But at the same time other ends have entered the scene, such as (1) winning the underdeveloped areas for the free world, (2) transforming traditional agriculture abroad, and (3) supporting and strengthening United States foreign policy in general.

---

[5]Fainsod, Gordon, and Palamountain, *Government and the American Economy*, p. 155; and Clair Wilcox, *Public Policies Toward Business*, 3rd ed. (Homewood: Richard D. Irwin, Inc., 1966), p. 785.

FARM EXPORT MARKETS

Pursuant to the Reciprocal Trade Agreements Act, the United States followed an increasingly liberal policy toward foreign trade. Other nations began to show an interest in international trade, and in 1948 the General Agreement on Tariffs and Trade (GATT) was created as an international organization for supervision and promotion of international trade and international trade agreements. Foreign trade in farm commodities was an important concern of GATT. Some sixty nations affiliated with GATT. This international institution has become a principal arena for negotiations, for lowering tariffs, for considering import quotas. Negotiated agreements, particularly import quotas, have been used to torpedo what may seem to be liberalizing policies in lower tariffs.[6]

GATT seeks to expand trade by removing or reducing trade barriers, especially tariffs. The United States has participated in these negotiations with increased energy since the enactment of the Trade Expansion Act of 1962. Foreign markets have been resistant to large increases in trading in farm products, as most developed countries have encouraged and protected domestic agriculture. Regional groupings, such as the European Common Market, also establish policies which may impede negotiations across their boundaries.

Although the agricultural sector has lagged behind the industrial in removing restrictions in international trade, the pressure for improving world markets has continued. With respect to the general operation of GATT, it has been concluded that

This international forum for the frank discussion of mutual problems has proved to be an effective way to develop good will and cooperation among nations in resolving problems of trade relations. Although originally intended as a stopgap, the GATT is the only instrument that provides a set of rules for international trade and the machinery to carry them out.[7]

---

[6]Richard de Felice, "General Agreement on Tariffs and Trade," *Farmer's World: Yearbook of U.S. Department of Agriculture, 1964* (Washington: U.S. Government Printing Office, 1964), pp. 476–81.
[7]*Ibid.*, p. 481.

Prior to and continuing after the enactment of GATT, the United States had been actively participating in international agreements seeking to rationalize trade in specific commodities. These commodity agreements were attempted in cases where competing producers posed some threat to world markets due to surpluses.

The contribution of foreign trade to solution of pressing problems, such as those besetting American agriculture, is yet to be assayed. The classic utility of trade as a vehicle of current economic growth is not realizable in any clear form because of the interposition of broad-scale and competitive "aid" programs, to which we shall presently turn. These latter policies constitute sets of empirical interventions predicated on political or ideological determinants rather than economic ones. Another practical difficulty in building effective trade relations is caused by the enormous and widening productivity gap between the United States economy and that of undeveloped areas.

Though our concern in this book is primarily centered on domestic aspects of change, the interrelation of contemporary agriculture with world affairs leads to noticing the consequences abroad as well as at home. It appears likely that liberalizing foreign aid policies has some facilitative effects only if basic social changes are brought about in the underdeveloped areas. Our arguments here would be based on the same underlying theses that have been used to explore American agrarianism: that basic social factors, including emphatically the ideological with the material, predetermine the behavior of the people. This may indicate a likelihood that efforts to pursue an outmoded course will be made; it does not, however, commit us to a blindly deterministic acceptance. The pleas from abroad for change now can be clearly heard. If evolution does not accelerate, revolutions now being attempted may run more violent courses.

In the nineteenth century, foreign trade succeeded in building modernized enclaves of agricultural-based export economies

surrounded by totally undeveloped and stagnant societies.[8]
This outcome is not entirely averted by aid programs, unless
domestic forces are released internally in local communities for
the purpose of effecting basic social changes. The domestic
forces we refer to are those located in the underdeveloped nations.

Domestically, the development of policies tending to increase
the outward flow of agricultural goods will provide incentive for
expanded production. Evidences are beginning to appear at the
time of this writing that interests are forming and vesting in the
functions that surround foreign trade and aid. Even as some
objectives are reached and some others are discovered to be
clearly unreachable, the policies and programs will continue on
an increasing scale. The interests in sending experts abroad,
drawn from the ranks of teachers, researchers and extension
specialists of the land-grant university, the USDA and other
agencies, also build up comparable on-going expectations, and the
anticipated effect will be to activate this field of training and
consequently enhance rather than deplete the supply. Foreign
aid programs are inextricably interwoven with foreign trade,
and the above considerations are relevant to the aspects of
foreign aid and credit to which we next turn.

PUBLIC LAW 480 AND PROJECT ASSISTANCE

In 1954, Congress passed the Agricultural Trade Development
and Assistance Act, known as P. L. 480. Of the several parts
of this law, the most important is one that permits the
government to negotiate an agreement with a foreign government
by which that government can buy surplus U. S. farm products
with its own currency. The credits in foreign currency are used
by the United States within the country; they may be lent to
the country for development purposes, they may be utilized
to pay for lecturers or research scholars under the State
Department program for exchange of persons, or they may be

[8]Gustav Ranis, *The United States and the Developing Economies*
(New York: W. W. Norton and Co., 1964), pp. 160-66.

used by the United States to pay costs related to the operation of the embassy in the country. During the first ten years of the Act, about six billion dollars' worth of foreign currency was acquired for economic development in developing nations.

Other provisions of the law provide for the donation of food to alleviate suffering from natural disaster or to help in refugee camps, and to grant surplus farm products to underdeveloped countries for use in welfare programs. Similar grants can be made to international organizations, and donations of surplus farm commodities can be made to nonprofit voluntary agencies for assistance to needy persons in foreign lands. A later amendment added an authorization to the Department of Agriculture to sell surplus commodities for credit in dollars repayable over a thirty-year period.

Export operations under P. L. 480 have become a factor of increasing importance in agricultural policy. Wheat, for example, had presented most difficult problems of surplus storage. Only after 1962 did the carryover in wheat begin to decline, but since that date a steady decline has taken place, from an average of 1,244,600,000 bushels in 1958–1962 to 819 million bushels for 1965 and to 536 million bushels for 1966. Since about 80 percent of the wheat exported, totaling over 700 million bushels per year, are under P. L. 480, it can be seen that this law has made a contribution to the solution of the marketing problems of at least one sector of commercial agriculture. If the wheat carryover continues to decline, the time may come when policy-makers will be confronted with the issue of increasing production to meet needs of a program which was originally attractive for its potential for reducing surplus storage problems. While the theoretical objections, particularly those made by economists, indicate that other methods might have had a more effective goal-maximization, the techniques used have been sufficient to implicate American agriculture in the fortunes of a number of foreign cultures. Thus a complicated series of reciprocal expectations has been built up.

Agriculture has been made a compelling actor in an increasingly interdependent world. In 1860 the American farmer was still a frontiersman; in 1960 he had become a figure in world politics.

Programs such as those authorized by P. L. 480 are classified as nonproject programs, designed to move resources directly into the economy of the receiving country through its own commercial channels. Not all of the nonproject assistance can be directly related to the agricultural sector of the American economy, but it is of direct relevance to agriculture inasmuch as it has been utilized as a prime mechanism for moving surplus products out of the U.S. domestic market.

Equally important to U. S. agriculture are several programs designated as the project type. These include the Technical Cooperation Administration, formed in 1950 in response to President Truman's inaugural address of 1949 containing the famous Point 4 appeal; the Mutual Security Agency, which underwent a number of administrative reorganizations to become in 1962 the Agency for International Development; and the numerous technical assistance projects under the "expanded programs" of the United Nations.

Project assistance is characterized by the use of professionals and technicians who are engaged by a contracting party under the terms of the agreed project. For example, an American university might contract with the Agency for International Development to provide the professional and technical services arrived at by negotiation between the U. S. Department of State and the appropriate office of the recipient country. The general objective of economic development indicates the major emphasis of this effort, with agricultural development occupying an important position. The AID has become the main governmental agency for project assistance; its work has included education of foreign students in American universities, scientific research in foreign countries in problems related to production of economic goods, and extension services in rural communities in backward areas.

The American land-grant universities, the extension service of the USDA, and the agricultural experiment stations provided a powerful alliance of institutions that has been called upon to provide personnel and technological experts for overseas projects. A majority of the sixty-five American universities holding AID contracts in 1962 were land-grant universities, and agricultural development occupied a high priority among the project designs. "With both private and state universities participating, university involvement in overseas educational programs grew so rapidly that by the 1950's, as E. D. Eddy has pointed out, 'the Land-Grant College idea had become world-wide.' "[9]

The exportability of the land-grant university concept with its huge production component is uncertain. The contrasting socioeconomic environments as between the United States and undeveloped areas are an unknown quantity. What has been accepted here as a desirable and tension-relieving direction of change is an innovation series completely unknown (hence unsettling) to peasant agriculture. The recognized need to prepare people for technical innovation calls for an applied social science which has not yet been developed.

PRIVATE FOUNDATIONS AND ORGANIZATIONS

Among the important vehicles for the export of U. S. agriculture, private philanthropists rival the federal government in initiative and energy. Endowed with a flexible and pragmatic approach, the private foundations are able and willing to respond to special needs. They are not closely confined by foreign policy requirements and commitments as are the federal agencies. They have more freedom of choice.

The Rockefeller Foundation has been engaged in foreign agriculture problems since 1924 and by 1964 had invested 66 million dollars in agricultural development.[10] During these forty years it has, on an increasing scale, developed such activities as supporting fellowships to foreign students for studying agriculture in the United States, establishing agricultural development programs in underdeveloped areas, and operating laboratories for research in scientific agriculture. A foremost example of the last-named is the International Rice Research Institute, located at Los Banos, Philippinés, the site of the Agricultural College

[9]Report of the *Committee on the University and World Affairs* (New York: Ford Foundation, 1960), p. 33.
[10]A. H. Moseman and F. F. Hill, "Private Foundations and Organizations," *Farmer's World: Yearbook of Agriculture, 1964*, p. 527.

of the University of the Philippines. The production problems of agriculture have engaged the attention of this foundation.

Beginning in 1952, the Ford Foundation has contributed heavily to foreign agricultural development, frequently collaborating with the Rockefeller Foundation to make a united effort on important projects. The construction of the International Rice Research Institute mentioned above was financed largely by the Ford Foundation, while the Rockefeller Foundation assumed the cost and responsibility for operation. Major categories of Ford Foundation work in agricultural development have been development of agricultural schools, scientific research in production and marketing, and village pilot and demonstration projects. Community development has received a substantial share of attention. In twelve years between 1952 and 1964, the Ford Foundation spent about 40 million dollars in various phases of foreign agricultural and village development. The Ford Foundation has placed a greater emphasis on farm problems other than production.

A number of private organizations, smaller in scope and budget than the two described above, are active in foreign agriculture. These include the Kellogg Foundation, established in 1953; the Agricultural Development Council, Inc., formerly the Council on Educational and Cultural Affairs, started in 1953; the International Development Services, also first organized in 1953; and the Cooperative for American Relief Everywhere (CARE), set up in 1945 to distribute food and clothing to war-devastated areas, later including farm tools and equipment and focusing on areas of subsistence agriculture. Typical of the many church-related agencies active in this area is the Church World Service, a cooperative effort on the part of a number of denominations to provide resources for introducing improved farming methods as well as to distribute surplus farm commodities. It will be noted that the post-World War II period has been the time in which many private ventures were initiated.

INTERNATIONAL ORGANIZATIONS

Commercial agriculture on the contemporary world scene, with United States agriculture in the vanguard but no longer alone,

bids to conquer one of mankind's most ancient enemies—
starvation. In the climate of a world concern for averting
international conflict, forty-four nations addressed themselves to
the problems of food and agriculture in a conference at Hot
Springs, Virginia, in the late spring of 1943. The organization
formed there became the Food and Agriculture Organization of
the United Nations in 1945, a prototype for several regional
organizations devoted to the same concern—promotion and
dissemination of the agricultural "revolution."

These agencies provide for an international exchange of
information and assistance. Although, in terms of the staggering
dimensions of the world food problem, the inadequacy of the
international budget for food and agriculture is starkly revealed,
an elaborate network of organization has been consistently
supported in servicing projects varying in length from a few
months to several years. An important facet of the work of FAO
has been providing technical personnel to impart their skills to
people where this knowledge is almost nonexistent.

A most important phase of FAO's program is that of collecting,
recording, and publishing information about world conditions
in food and agriculture. Included are "yearbooks of production
and trade statistics; technical and scientific publications . . .;
reports of missions and experts serving on technical assistance
projects; reports on training centers and technical and economic
meetings; and reports on sessions of the FAO Conference and
Council."[11]

The basic and pervasive nature of the work of FAO encourages
close cooperation with other international organizations. Some
of these are the United Nations Educational, Scientific, and
Cultural Organization (UNESCO); the Expanded Program of
Technical Assistance (EPTA); the United Nations Special Fund
(UNSF); and many others, including the many regional
organizations and branches.[12]

---

[11]Ralph W. Phillips and Kenneth A. Haines, "FAO of the United
Nations," *Farmer's World: The Yearbook of Agriculture, 1964*, p. 43.
[12]The regional organizations in food and agriculture include the Inter-
American Institute of Agricultural Sciences (IAIAS), the European

An upward swing of activities has characterized FAO during
the 1960's, both in data collecting and in technical and
educational undertakings.

THE RECIPIENT SYSTEMS

It has become apparent that the end of World War II marks the
start of an era of struggle and strife that is properly described
as a global revolution in a socio-political context. The essence
of this effort at what Heilbroner terms "The Great Ascent"[13] is
difficult to capture in words. The drive for economic development
has been accepted in some quarters as an essentially technological
process; however, this misses an important center of the problem:
the replacing of institutionalized values which have over a long
time controlled the behavior of individuals in their social settings.
Heilbroner cautions that "we deceive ourselves when we think of
economic development in the pallid terms of economics alone."[14]

An approach to the basic nature of the conflict was made by Lin
Piao, China's Minister of National Defense, when he described
the global revolution as a struggle between the rural (Afro-Asian)
and the urban (Euro-American) parts of the world.[15] While
this division contradicts conventional definitions of "rural" and
"urban," it delineates in proximate terms a great cleavage
otherwise described as the division between "haves" and
"have-nots." In the setting of trans-national transactions, the
dominant forces of the West appear to be specialized,
technological, and commercial—hence urban. On this front,
commercial farmers readily occupy an important sector. Viewing
the elements involved in the struggle for development, the
motley and variegated peoples arrayed on the Afro-Asian side
display traditional, only slightly mechanized, and agrarian

Productivity Agency (EPA), Committee on Food and Agriculture of
the Organization for European Economic Cooperation (OEEC), and
the Commission for a Common Agricultural Policy of the Common
Market.
[13]Robert L. Heilbroner. *The Great Ascent* (New York: Harper
and Row, 1963).
[14]*Ibid.*, p. 24.
[15]*U.S. News and World Report* (Oct. 25, 1965), 42.

characteristics. The existence of the great cities of that part of the world does not impair this interpretation; these cities have been accurately characterized as "huge clusters of rural villages."

In the Afro-Asian world there is, however, a thin veneer that is urban, although pertaining to only a minute percent of the population. Though few in number, the persons with qualities here designated as urban constitute the oligarchies which are at the peaks of the social and governmental organizations of the cultures of this part of the world.[16]

Thus, some great areas of decision-making in developing areas, e.g., national state decisions, decisions of the large units of commerce and business, and in some cases religious affairs, are dominated by decision-makers who are quite at home with modern concepts. A part of the problem of developmental change is to be found in the wide gap between the public decision-makers and their people who live in the traditionalism of rural villages. Inevitably, vested interests develop in the status quo, part of which may consist of material benefits that assume important dimensions.

It is ironic that the state policies of presumably urbanized America are more directly conditioned by agrarian influences than are those of developing areas. For part of the explanation, we return to such causes as rural overrepresentation in American legislatures; long tenure in office of rural legislators with attendant rise to powerful committee chairmanships; and the perpetuation of the agrarian mythology in the forms traced in earlier chapters of this work.

A partial explanation of the paradox suggested by the preceding paragraphs lies of course in the open channels of communications and freedom and equality (democracy in general) in American society, whereas in the developing areas effective communication (and voting) does not exist—decision-makers are not accountable

---

[16]The relation of these oligarchies to the heads of states throws light on the status of agriculture in developing nations. By indirection, it further illuminates the agrarian scene in America. This is particularly true in situations where the head of state has become, by popular election or otherwise, a charismatic champion of the masses.

to the farmers and workers. In such matters as withholding reapportionment, the democratic process operates to flout democratic principles; in developing areas, the undemocratic status quo is maintained by quite the opposite kind of processes. When state and national policies of the United States are carried abroad as technical and agricultural aid programs, they inevitably carry with them the part of agrarian ideology that is imbedded in the infrastructure of commercial agriculture. The part of the ideology that is left behind, the immobile traditional agriculture, contains the key to understanding foreign systems. Without this understanding complications ensue.

One of the expressions of the optimism of the American spirit is found in the implicit faith revealed by the terms "emerging," "developing areas," and "transitional societies." These terms have, however, helped to obscure meaningful differences; they imply a common direction, if not a common condition, and similar stages or processes of change. These differences tend to become unmanageable when put in Heilbroner's terms: "Variations in climate and resources—compounded by variations in local customs and institutions—make of the actual work of development a many-faceted rather than a universally similar task . . ." As Paul Hoffman, Director of the United Nations Special Fund, has summarized it succinctly: 'A hundred nations, a hundred problems.' "[17]

Between unmanageable variety and misleading uniformity, it is possible to sort out types of foreign agriculture of significance to our own interests and capable of shedding light on the ideological, theoretical, and practical aspects of agriculture and social change in general. These classes or types are (1) commercial, (2) peasant, and (3) primitive, or slash-and-burn, agriculture.[18]

---

[17]Heilbroner, *The Great Ascent*, p. 47. The extensive omission in this quotation takes some liberty with the composition but does not alter the meaning.

[18]We do not deal categorically with collective agriculture. This constitutes an important mode of organization to which we may attend in future work on international agriculture.

Commercial Agriculture

It was noted earlier in this chapter that the United States is not alone in its ability or in its efforts to supply agricultural assistance to other nations. Though the United States is in the forefront with its prodigious productive powers, other nations, too, have forged keys to commercial agriculture. How the forces of change operate, where the pains and wounds are, who are the beneficiaries, are great questions in each case. These are open and debated subjects in the United States, as voluminous pages of the *Congressional Record* attest, and the final answers cannot be expected soon.

Not all commercial agriculture is export market agriculture. Nor is it necessarily a large-scale agriculture. Great Britain's agriculture represents a high degree of commercialization with heavy imports and a stable number of small farms.[19] The very generous subsidization of British farmers directed toward maximum efficiency in production indicates a public opinion that agriculture is indispensable to the welfare of a highly industrialized society. No doubt this opinion is strengthened by the remarkably effective interest group, the Farmers Union. In any case, it appears that were it not for subsidies, England would entirely quit the business of commercial agriculture. Agriculture appears much like metropolitan transit services, or other public utilities, unable to operate as independent economic units, yet considered indispensable to the welfare of the community.

Public policy in Britain supports commercial agriculture, at the insistence of the Farmers Union, at a high level of technical and productive efficiency. There may be an unintended farsightedness in this policy if demands for food and fibre increase due to population increase and improved living standards.

Agriculture is moving or is movable into commercial modernization throughout most of western Europe. Against a

---

[19]Merlin Gustafson, "Freedom and Planning in British Agriculture," *The Midwest Quarterly* (Autumn 1963), 33–47. For an extended treatment, see Peter Self and H. J. Storing, *The State and the Farmer* (London: G. Allen & Unwin, Ltd., 1962).

background of a strong peasant tradition, this kind of change was almost imperceptible except for the Scandinavian countries down to 1940. The changes now under way are formulated and executed by positive state action. State action, in turn, has become coordinated in multilateral policies through the use of the Common Market. The Treaty of Rome in 1957 made a common agricultural policy an essential goal. Article 40, par. 1, states that: "Member States shall gradually adopt the common agricultural policy during the transitional period and shall establish it not later than the end of that period." The common agricultural policy (CAP) was adopted in the Brussels agreement of 1962.

France offers a good example of the national objectives and achievements of a nation's agriculture.[20] Gross labor productivity in French agriculture has grown 7 percent annually during the 60's, reflecting a basic objective of emerging societies. The basic factors in this modernization are mechanization, fertilizers, and growth of applied agricultural research. Sales of tractors increased in France from 29,150 in 1952 to 112,300 in 1957, typical of the rapid trend toward mechanized agriculture. Improvement in rural living conditions is realized through programs of electrification, road construction, water facilities development, and rural housing. Scientific and technical facilities in agriculture are being expanded as indicated by an expansion in the staff of the National Institute for Agronomic Research from 294 to 3,290 persons. The gains made by French agriculture have been impressive. However, Wright's description of the transition manifests the costs and benefits of directed change in agriculture.

Facing redoubtable difficulties, both physical and social, Japanese agriculture furnishes another example of modernization. Here again, the change is linked directly to national policy and correlates directly with the growth of democracy in Japan. The concern of the Japanese government for agricultural production

---

[20]Information provided by the *Service de presse et d'information*, 972 Fifth Ave., New York. See also Gordon Wright, *Rural Revolution in France* (Stanford: Stanford University Press, 1964).

reflects a motivation similar to that of England—a determination to maintain maximum output of food and fibre products in a predominantly industrialized economy.

A summary of the 1964 White Paper on Agriculture points out that

Labor productivity per person on Japanese farms rose by 30 percent during the five-year period prior to 1963 (an annual increase rate of 5.5 percent). Although this 30 percent increase rate still stands in sharp contrast to the 51 percent increase rate registered in manufacturing productivity for the same five year period, it is nevertheless a remarkable development considering the natural limitations imposed upon agriculture in Japan. At the same time, this rate is comparable to that in any other industrialized country.[21]

The White Paper reports that the percent of employed persons engaged in agriculture declined from 37.1 in 1955 to 25.9 in 1963. As in the case of agriculture in the United States, Japanese agriculture has made a large contribution to the industrial labor force. Other contributions resemble the United States case: a market for industrial goods and an increase in the supply of agricultural products for urban consumers. A food deficit country, Japan has pressed for a modernized agriculture which has held food imports stable with rising standards of consumption. Thus, a large share of the world food supply has been available for consumption elsewhere as a result of Japan's agricultural modernization.

Other examples of commercial agriculture outside the United States are available. These examples show that our experience is not unique. They encourage study as difficulties and resistances to development are encountered. We have not included examples of modernizing agriculture under collective or socialist auspices, though there are many collective agricultural systems that are striving for modernization, including, in addition to the Soviet forms of Russia, mainland China, and central Europe, the smaller units of Israeli agriculture.

---

[21]Summary provided by the Japan Information Service.

Peasant Agriculture

To look at the spread and growth of modernization in agriculture encourages the false view that this is a universal phenomenon and the transition is inevitable in the course of time. This view would hold that the only direction of change is toward modernization. The contemporary demands for modernization are stronger and more articulate than they have ever been; both the incentives for change and the instruments for bringing modernization about are admittedly impressive. The situation, however, is neither as simple nor as hopeful as it appears. To a large extent, the national agricultures that are modernizing are special cases, beyond the degree to which all economies are special cases.

Notwithstanding the entry of modernization into some agricultural economies in replacement of peasant agriculture, the predominant agriculture of the world is yet that of the peasant village. The emergent examples cited above are advanced in their conversion processes, but the task has not been completed. In other cases, such as the Philippines, valiant efforts have been made, with results that indicate the level of difficulty of the undertaking.

Peasant agriculture has several characteristics that deserve consideration in the context of this work. First, more of the world's farmers follow this way of life than any other. American technical aid projects abroad are certain to encounter the peasant system.

Second, it is not to be confused with primitive, or subsistence agriculture. Peasants constitute the "mud-sill" class that partially supports an elaborate and a costly class system, the town life of which it is a part, and usually teeming cities which its people fear.[22] Complicated systems of ownership and rights exist in the peasant culture.

Third, it is an inert and unproductive form of economy. In some cases it is so unproductive that it can hardly be said that there

---

[22]There are, in world history, striking cases of wealthy peasants. These are, at least, exceptional phenomena.

is an economy. Little of the social, governmental, and business infrastructure that marks the emergent society is to be found. However, there is a margin of production above subsistence that keeps the system going—where the peasant family gives up half of what they raise to their landlord the margin appears substantial. We choose to describe the peasant system, as inert rather than with the more conventional term static, the latter indicating, apparently, no motion or direction of any kind. There are, of course, movements, even changes, in peasant communities. One kind of change is the cyclical pattern elicited by the seasons —rainy and dry, hot and cold. These are compounded by the need to adjust to the unusual but recurring natural phenomena —the years the monsoon fails, the periodic catastrophe in typhoon, earthquake, or volcanic eruption. The other kind of change is the kind of linear progression as the peasant society becomes more peasant-like. The obligations of the semi-feudal order are complicated—these develop and elaborate over time. Landlords change, as from church to corporation, or even from father to son. The changes can well be in the direction of more and more refinements in the class system, subsistence peasantry, folklore and ceremonialism in the social life and customs. These changes may be away from, rather than toward, "modernization." These changes do not bespeak development, unless by accident. Nor are they self-directed. They are best described as inertia— a kind of momentum but not the "momentum of rising expectations."

A fourth characteristic is the peasant personality and temperament as delineated by an anthropologist: "It logically follows, however, the empirically observable inertness of peasant society. This trait is the peasants' feeling of impotence in the face of the outside world."[23] From this come the well-known spirit of fatalism, the tendency toward improvidence, the lack of a social concern beyond the immediate family.

---

[23]George M. Foster, *Traditional Cultures and the Impact of Technological Change* (New York: Harper and Brothers, 1962), pp. 47–48.

It is easy to assume a totally critical pose toward the peasantry from outside peasant culture. Yet, given the situation in which the young peasant farmer finds himself, there is much reason to commend him for the way in which he absorbs the experience of past generations. The lessons of destitution and exploitation have been learned. This is a way of life that allows for survival and little more. To change would be to plunge into an unknown and highly dangerous set of conditions.

It has been said that the American, having had no experience in a feudal or peasant society, cannot conceptualize the meaning of this way of life. It is outside the realm of our experience and understanding. It may, nonetheless, be possible, by empirical procedures, to determine how much of our stereotype of peasant society is accurate. We now have a substantial backlog of studies in anthropology and sociology on the subject.[24] We know the dangers of overgeneralization. Beyond the basic similarities above, a tremendous variety exists among the different national and geographical areas. These variations attach themselves to all aspects of life—the material, associational, religious, recreational, and so forth.

Given the insistence, both within and without, that an age of modernization, meaning mechanization and Westernization, be ushered in, peasant agriculture must be perceived as one of the world's great problem areas—pressing the West for solution.

Primitive Agriculture

Peasant agriculture is not primitive; in Asia, rich lowlands are tilled by poor peasants while verdant mountains are abodes for primitive agriculturists, even poorer in worldly goods and security. Poor as it is, peasant agriculture supports itself and contributes to city life, a national government, and tax-evading landlords. Primitive agriculture does none of these.

---

[24]Robert Redfield, *Peasant Society and Culture* (Chicago: University of Chicago Press, 1956); Edward C. Banfield, *The Moral Basis of a Backward Society* (Glencoe, Ill.: Free Press, 1958); Henry Habib Ayrout, *The Egyptian Peasant* (Boston: Beacon Press, 1963).

A description of the Garos, a tribe living in southwestern Assam, in Southeast Asia, typifies this way of life:

Each year the Garos clear a new patch of land and let it dry until the end of March, when they burn the cuttings which they have left scattered about. The planting is begun early in the morning after the fire, for the Garos feel that it must be done while the blackened ash can still blow over the seeds and promote their growth. Many of the crops are planted by broadcasting. Instead of planting each crop in its own separate plot, the farmer deliberately mixes the seeds of all species before he scatters them about the fields . . . As a result millet, maize, taro, yams, chilipeppers, cotton, ginger and a score of other foods come up thoroughly intermixed. . . . When the cotton (the last crop to ripen) has been harvested, the fields are cleaned once again.

The next year the fields are used exclusively for rice, the only proper staple and an essential part of every meal . . . The rice is usually harvested in September. . . . No more crops are grown on them for eight or ten years, when the cycle is repeated.[25]

This semi-sedentary agriculture is typical of most of the mountain country in Southeast Asia and is found in many parts of the world. The Philippines, not uniquely, represent simultaneously commercial, peasant, and primitive, or "slash-and-burn," agriculture. The powerful commercial agriculture may in time displace the others, a process not quite the same as changing a community, by technical aid and extension services, from one way of life to another.

SUMMARY

The involvement of American agriculture in foreign policies and problems is far-reaching in its implications and consequences. The power of technology applied to farm production has contributed greatly to freeing human energy for industrial growth. The resulting growth of an urbanized society permeated with agrarian values, made possible by a low ratio of people to land, is not likely to be repeated elsewhere. Our foreign

---

[25]Robbins Burling, *Hill Farms and Padi Fields: Life in Mainland Southeast Asia* (New York: Prentice-Hall, 1965), pp. 41–42.

agriculture programs have contributed to further mechanizing and "scientizing" American agriculture, a change more appropriately considered a momentum in one direction than a basic social change; whether similar forces can give foreign agricultural systems this direction remains to be determined in most cases.

Application of modern scientific techniques to agriculture is proceeding apace in many places outside the United States. In important cases, these are not nations that enter the export market with agricultural products. However, their contribution may, nonetheless, be significant in their addition to world food supply. Their contribution to scientific techniques and their experiments with guiding change in a variety of cultures may fill critical needs in meeting the rising expectations of the agricultural revolution.

From the point of view of this study, the effect on American agriculture of its venturing abroad is of much consequence. Land-grant universities, not long since locked in rural parochialism, have become centers of international activities. The farmer is made aware of his international role by the job of the Peace Corps in rural areas, by the International Farm Youth Exchange (IFYE), by P. L. 480 "markets," and many other activities. American agriculture and its farmers are being offered a role in the drama of world affairs. It is consequential that all of the doors opened thus far have been to the commercial farmers and farm experts who are least likely to have a fund of knowledge and insight into peasant or primitive agriculture and their attendant conditions.

The implicit exploitation of the peasant system and the instability of primitive agriculture are under pressure from external forces. The results of these pressures depend on the response from within the societies for the direction they will take. It cannot be assumed that the trail blazed by American agriculture will be followed by others without coercion. Rather, the more general optimism of America's first great Agrarian more appropriately describes our own: "Nothing then is unchangeable but the inherent and unalienable rights of man."

INDEX

Agency for International Development, 175
Agrarianism, 3–10, 15, 19–23, 26–37, 39, 40, 42, 43, 54, 61, 62, 65, 68, 75, 76, 77, 80, 81, 84, 85, 87, 90–93, 95–99, 101, 102, 104–107, 110–114, 128–131, 139, 142, 144, 146, 151, 152, 155, 170, 172, 180, 181, 188, 189
Agribusiness Concept, 55, 56
Agricultural College of the University of the Philippines, 176, 177
Agricultural Development Council, Inc., 177
Agricultural Marketing Act, 167
Agricultural transition (transformation), v, vi, vii, viii, 4, 6, 9, 10, 40, 41, 47, 51, 53, 63, 64, 72, 73, 77, 80, 82, 85, 92, 95, 102, 113, 115, 116, 120, 143, 150, 157, 175, 179, 180, 182–189; see also Industrialization, Urbanization
Agricultural types: refuge or venture, 132, 133, 134, 135, 138, 139, 140, 142, 143, 144, 146, 148, 149, 151, 152, 153, 154, 155, 156, 157, 158, 160, 163, 164; see also Rationality
Agricultural Wheel, 41
Alabama, 91
Alger, Bruce R., 103
Amelioration (ameliorative or supportive institutions), 8, 21, 31, 43–47, 61, 65, 120, 146, 154, 158
American Farm Bureau Federation (Farm Bureau), 41, 58, 59, 60, 66, 67, 70, 71, 82, 83n., 98, 99, 147
American Utopian Experiments, 14
Appalachia, 82, 84, 100, 118
Appalachia Redevelopment Act, 100
Area Redevelopment Acts, 100
Australia, 49

Bank of the United States, 31
Baruch, Bernard, 38
Bell, Daniel, 12, 13, 16
Bensman, Joseph, 69, 80, 84
Boulding, Kenneth, 72, 157–158
Brooke Farm, 14
Brown, Charles H., 103
Bryan, William Jennings, 96
Bureau of Agricultural Economics, 66
Burling, Robbins, 188

California's Central Valley, 66
Census of Agriculture, 124, 138, 148
Census of Population, 108
Central Europe, 184
China, 5, 6, 179, 184
Church World Service, 177
Civil War, 28, 41, 43, 47, 56, 58, 105, 147
Collective agriculture, vii, 184
Collectivism, corporate, empirical, 37, 39
College of Agriculture, University of Wisconsin, 47
Commodity Credit Corporation, 169

Commodity groups, 63, 147
Common agricultural policy (CAP), 183
Community differentiation, 63–72, 75, 76
Congressional Record, 102, 182
Constitutional Union Party, 58
Consumers Cooperative Association of Kansas City, Missouri (CCA), 62, 63
Cooperative Extension Services, 66
Cooperative for American Relief Everywhere (CARE), 177
Cooperative Marketing Act, 61
Cooperatives, 60–63, 76, 147, 148, 155, 167
Cotton, Norris, 103
Council on Educational and Cultural Affairs, 177
Country Life Commission, 45–46, 47, 61, 120, 154
Country Life movement, 58, 115, 147
County extension agent, 59, 61, 64, 70
Cuba, vi
Czechoslovakia, vii

Davis, Kingsley, 49
de Felice, Richard, 171
Democracy, vi, 29, 30, 31, 34, 35, 180, 181; *see also* Equality, Legislative reapportionment
Democratic party, 6, 57, 58, 99
Demographic characteristics or composition, 9, 49–50, 54, 106, 107, 108, 109, 121, 123, 124, 125, 126, 127, 133, 134, 137, 139, 163
Denmark, 49
Depression, 57, 64, 65, 107, 149, 168

Derge, David R., 91, 93
de Tocqueville, Alexis, 37, 162
Douglas, Paul, 101, 102, 103, 104
Dualistic pattern, 142

Eastern Europe, 6
Eddy, E. H., 176
Edwards, Everett E., 43
Eighteenth century, vii
Eisenhower, Dwight D., 100, 101, 103
Equality, 32, 64, 84, 94, 102
Equity movements, 41
European Common Market, 171, 183
Expanded Program of Technical Assistance (EPTA), 178
Experiment Stations, 44, 161, 175
Extension education system, 58
Extension service(s), 44, 47, 59, 68, 69, 70, 71, 100, 101, 104, 153, 157, 159, 161, 175, 188

Farm Holiday Association, 57
Farm Security Act, 99
Farm Security Administration, 65, 66, 76, 99n.
Farmer as victim, 110, 111, 113, 114, 116, 120, 128, 129, 130, 153
Farmers Alliances, 41, 114
Farmers Cooperative Association, 42
Farmers Educational and Cooperative Union of America (Farmers Union), 41, 57, 58, 99, 148
Farmer's Union (British), 182
Federal Farm Board, 61, 65, 167
Federal Reserve Bank, 44
Feed Grains Act, 100
Ferguson, Clarence M., 101
Festinger, Leon, 17, 18, 22

Firey, Walter, 52
Fisher, John, 79
Food and Agricultural Organization of the United Nations (FAO), 178, 179
Ford Foundation, 177
Foreign Aid, PL 480, project assistance, 173–175, 181, 185, 188
Foreign policy, marketing, tariffs, 31, 38, 39, 164, 165, 166, 167, 168, 169, 170–174, 176, 188
Foster, George, 161, 186
4-H Club, 119, 120
France, 25, 183
Frontier, 26, 27, 37, 110, 113, 118, 119, 153
Fundamentalism, 3, 28, 29, 37, 46, 54, 72, 95, 96, 102, 111, 112, 119, 128, 129, 130, 132, 151, 152, 154

Gallaher, Art, Jr., vii-viii, 69–70, 70
Galpin, Josiah, 47
Garos, 188
General Agreement on Tariffs and Trade (GATT), 171–172
Genung, A.B., 64
Goldschmidt, Walter, 66, 159
Goldsmith, Oliver, vi, vii
Goldwater, Barry, 141
Grain Futures Act, 167
Grange, 41, 42, 56, 57, 60, 114
Great Britain, 25, 182, 184
Great Plains, 34, 57, 83, 86n., 119, 123, 157
Griswold, A. Whitney, 29–30, 30–31
Gruen, Victor, 35
Grumm, John, 92, 93

Hadwiger, Don F., 51, 52
Haines, Kenneth A., 178

Hamilton, C. Horace, 75
Hammond, Bray, 34-35
Heilbroner, Robert L., 179, 181
Henderson, John, 101
High Plains of Texas, 52
Hoffman, Paul, 181
Hofstadter, Richard, 15, 16, 17
Homestead Act, 43, 157
Huntley, Chet, 73, 74, 75

Ideology (ideological expression, symbolic system), 11–23, 26, 28, 33, 35, 40, 62, 95, 97, 99, 112, 141, 142, 150, 162, 172; disconfirmation of, 17, 18, 22, 23, 112, 116, 150; see also Agrarianism
Illinois, 91
Independence (of farmer), 3, 28, 34, 36, 39, 42, 43, 46, 51, 54, 56, 111, 112, 114, 128, 129, 130, 144, 149, 152
Individualism, see Independence
Industrialization (industrial transition), v, vi, 4, 6, 7, 8, 9, 12, 13, 15, 19, 20, 22, 27, 28, 35, 40, 53, 60, 75, 106, 113, 115, 120, 121, 143, 152, 156, 158, 159, 161, 165, 188
Infrastructure, 120, 140, 143, 146, 147, 148, 149, 150, 154, 155, 157, 159, 162, 163, 181, 186; see also Land-grant System, United States Department of Agriculture, Country Life Movement, Organizations
Integration, horizontal and/or vertical, 55, 163, 164
Interdependence: international, 174; rural-industrial, 51, 53, 56; rural-urban, 23, 34, 36,

49, 51, 52, 73, 92, 104,
111, 113, 114, 118, 119,
127, 145
International agriculture, 5–6; *see
also* Foreign aid, foreign
policy
International Development Services, 177
International Farm Youth Exchange (IFYE), 189
International Rice Research Institute, 176, 177
Interstate Commerce Commission, 44
Israel, 184

Japan, 183, 184
Jefferson, Thomas, 3, 4, 7, 16,
25–26, 28, 30, 32, 33, 34,
35, 37, 46, 57, 74, 86, 90,
116, 189
Johnstone, Paul H., 28, 38, 39–
40, 45
Jones, Arthur R., Jr., 75

Kansas, 7, 29, 42, 74, 86*n*., 87,
87*n*., 91, 92, 94, 106,
109, 110, 112–113, 114,
115, 117, 118, 119, 120,
121, 123, 124, 127,
128, 132, 133, 134, 135,
136, 137, 138, 139, 152
154
Kansas State Board of Agriculture, 41, 44, 105, 107, 110,
111
Kansas State University, 74, 106
Kellogg Foundation, 177
Kennedy, John F., 103
Kerr, Clark, et al., 5, 51
Knight, Willis R., 38
Knutson, Coya, 103
Kraenzel, Carl F., 119

Laissez-faire, vii, 33, 34, 61, 156

Lake States Cut-over region,
121, 136
Lancaster, Lane, 85
Land, The, 73—74
Land-grant system, 39, 44, 46, 58,
59, 68, 71, 72, 73, 74,
76, 99, 116, 117, 118,
120, 147, 148, 150, 160,
161, 162, 173, 175,
176, 189
Land Use Planning, 66, 67, 68,
76
Legislative reapportionment, 5,
6, 23, 36*n*., 54, 83*n*., 85,
91, 93, 145, 181
Levinson, Daniel, 20
Lin Piao, 179
Lipset, S. M., 12, 13
Lord, Russell, 68
Luddite, 9

McConnell, Grant, 58, 70, 76
McNary-Haugen bill, 167
Malapportionment, gerrymander, 54, 90, 91, 93,
155, 157, 158–159, 180; *see
also* Democracy, Legislative
reapportionment
Management (as factor in modern
farming), 40, 55, 155
Mannheim, Karl, 11, 19, 19*n*.
Martin, Roscoe C., 81–82, 85
Maryland, 77, 121
Massachusetts, 109, 110, 112,
114, 117, 118, 119, 120,
121, 123, 132, 151
Massachusetts State Board of
Agriculture, 44, 105, 107,
110, 111
Mead, George Herbert, 20, 21,
157
Meader, George, 104
Merton, Robert K., 18
Midwest, 83, 157
Miller, Cecil, 18, 19

Miner, 66
Missouri, 91
Montana, 73
Moral virtue (attached to farm-
    ing) 3, 25–26, 29, 30,
    46, 112, 128, 129, 130,
    140, 146, 152
Moore, Wilbert E., 19, 20
Morrill Act, 157
Mount Weather Agreement, 66
Mutual Security Agency, 175
Mysliveček, Fr., vii

National Broadcasting Company,
    73
National Farmers Organization,
    (NFO), 57
National Institute for Agronomic
    Research (France), 183
Near East, 6
Nelson, Lowry, vi, 52
New Deal, 96, 97, 99, 160
New England and Western farm-
    ing; see Massachusetts,
    Kansas
New Harmony, 14
New Zealand, 49
Nineteenth century (as era in
    American agriculture), 29,
    37, 40, 41, 44, 45, 96,
    105, 110, 111, 147, 172
Non-Partisan League, 58
North Dakota, 58, 99

Organizations or associations, 33,
    41–43, 46, 51–63, 64,
    70, 76, 98, 113, 114–115,
    120, 141–142, 143, 147,
    150, 154, 155, 157, 159–
    161, 162–164, 174, 180;
    see also specific organizations
Ozark-Appalachian Highlands,
    121, 136

Packers and Stockyards Act, 167

Peace Corps, 189
Peasant agriculture, v, 161, 176,
    181, 185, 186, 187, 188,
    189
Persistence (perseverance), 10
Philippines, 86, 176, 185, 188
Phillips, Ralph W., 178
Plainville, vii, 69, 70
Pluralism, 83, 84, 85, 102
Poland, 168
Political behavior, 99; see also
    Democratic party, Republi-
    can party, Populist party,
    Public sector
Population, movement or change,
    v, 9, 22, 38, 45, 49–50, 73,
    85, 88, 107, 109, 117,
    118, 127, 128, 131, 134,
    144, 145, 153, 154
Populist party, 41, 45, 107,
    114
Primitive (subsistence) agricul-
    ture, 181, 185, 187, 188,
    189
Private sector, 32–35, 63, 66,
    71, 81, 82, 83, 92, 154, 155,
    160, 164, 165
Produce Agency Act, 167
Public sector (federal, state, or
    local government), 27, 31–
    32, 34, 35, 52, 63, 64,
    66, 69, 70, 71, 79, 80,
    82, 83, 84, 85, 89, 90, 91,
    92, 93, 94, 95, 96, 97,
    99, 154, 155, 157, 158, 160,
    164, 165, 180; see also Poli-
    tical behavior, specific poli-
    tical parties

Railroads, 36, 38, 41, 43
Ranis, Gustav, 173
Rasmussen, Wayne D., 68
Rationality (as characteristic of
    modern farmers), 39, 69;
    rational and traditional

farmers, 80, 81, 83, 106, 132, 140

Raup, Philip M., 53

Reciprocal Trade Agreements Act, 168, 171

Republican party, 13, 57, 99, 100

Resettlement Administration, 65

Riecken, Henry W., 17, 18, 22

Rockefeller Foundation, 176, 177

Roosevelt, Franklin, 141

Rural Area Development, 68

Rural Development, 68, 76

Rural Electrification Administration, 37, 61

Rural Poverty Programs, 68

Ruttan, Vernon W., 53

Scandinavia, 183

Schachter, Stanley, 17, 18, 22

Schulze, Rolf, 15*n*.

Selznick, Philip, 11

Shakers, 14

Sherman Antitrust Act, 44

Sjoberg, Gideon, 27

Smith, Howard R., 36

Smith-Lever Act, 59

Social change, vi, 5, 19, 21, 22, 30, 33, 116, 150, 151, 156, 157, 158, 162, 172, 181, 186, 189; costs and benefits of, 7, 73, 143, 144, 183; and educational institutions, 87, 117, 140, 144, 153; social responses to, 150

Social Darwinism, 14, 15, 16

Social differentiation, 84, 106, 142, 154, 156

Soil-Bank, 100

Southeast Asia, 188

Soviet Union, 5, 6, 8, 170, 184

Spanish or Continental influence on governmental systems, 86

State Department, 173, 175

Subsidization, 64, 182

Surplus production, v, vii

Taylor, Carl, 41, 44

Taylor, Lee, 175

Taylor, John, 16, 31–32, 33, 34, 35

Technical Cooperation Administration, 175

Technical experts, 6, 7, 70, 77, 89, 173

Technocracy, 14

Tennessee Valley Authority (TVA), 11–12*n*.

Tennessee Valley Authority Act, 100

The Land, 73–74

Time (as factor in transition), 10, 113, 157, 158

Trade Expansion Act, 171

Treaty of Rome, 183

Truesdell, Leon E., 108

Truman, Harry S, 175

Tunnard, Christopher, 35

Turner, Frederick Jackson, 37

Twentieth century, 40, 56, 60

United Nations Educational, Scientific, and Cultural Organization (UNESCO), 178

United Nations Special Fund (UNSF), 178, 181

United States Department of Agriculture (USDA), 43, 46, 61, 65, 66, 67, 70, 100, 120, 169, 173, 174, 175

United States Supreme Court, 6, 36*n*., 54, 56, 83*n*., 93, 94, 95, 95*n*.

Urbanization, v, 4, 9, 20, 27, 28, 35, 37, 57, 75, 90, 91, 121, 143, 156, 166

Utopian Socialism, 14

Venture and refuge farmers, *see* Agricultural types

Vidich, Arthur J., 69, 80, 84
Virginia, 91
Vocational agriculture, 47
von Martin, Alfred, 11

Warren, Earl, Chief Justice of
    the Supreme Court, 6, 93–
    94
Welfare State, 12, 14, 16
West, James, 69
    (Japan), 184

Williams, Robin M., Jr., 163
Wilson, C. Peairs, 72
Wisconsin, 60
World War I, 4, 38–39, 41, 47,
    58, 64, 105, 108, 147,
    155, 165
World War II, 67, 148, 168,
    169, 170, 172
Wright, Frank Lloyd, 35

Zeigler, Harmon, 98